Self-T

2 In 1

Hidden Tools To Quiet The Voice In Your Head, Get Your Life Moving Forward And Find Happiness

By

Stuart Wallace

Table of Contents

The Self Talk Solution

The Power Of Self-Talk

Chapter 5: Self-Talk For Business Success 221

Chapter 6: Positive Self-Talk For Social Relations 252

The Self-Talk Solution

The Proven Concept Of Breaking Free From Intense Negative Thoughts To Never Feel Weak Again

By

Stuart Wallace

Introduction

Are you hounded by relentless thoughts about how you are a failure, or how you screwed up yet again, or how you are not good enough? Are you tired of being depressed, anxious, and full of self-blame? Do you lie awake at night, thinking horrible things about yourself? Have your relationships or even your health suffered as a result of your persistent unhappy thinking?

I understand your fear that you will never be happy again. For months or even years, perhaps for your whole life, you have been unhappy. Your head is full of ugly thoughts that promptly obliterate any joy you do experience. What you are suffering from is negative self-talk.

You can and will feel happiness again. The reason why is that your mind is malleable and you can restructure your self-talk to bring about more positivity. This process does not happen overnight. It requires some effort on your part and a series of psychologist-formulated techniques that you will learn in the following pages.

This book is not just another "Be Happy" listicle. I read plenty of those listicles when I was struggling with low self-esteem and depression, and while the advice contained in them was usually sensible, they never did much good. This is because they didn't teach the fundamentals of self-talk psychology and how to get to the root of the habits that drive negative self-talk.

When I was finally fed up with being unhappy, I sought the help of cognitive behavioral therapy. I learned that I could perform many techniques on my own without an expensive therapist, so I set about finding the best techniques that actually offered me relief. After consulting a myriad of psychology journals and CBT guides, I finally found a solution to my poor thinking habits. Now I am here to present my findings to you.

Your self-talk drives how you think, feel, and act. It is the linguistic instructions that your mind gives to you as you go about your day. When you change your self-talk to something positive, you will see every area of your life change for the better. You will start to see the good in yourself, and you will start to love yourself. You will be able to forgive and fix your mistakes. People will start to enjoy being around you more, so your relationships will improve and you will make more friends. As you enrich your career with enthusiasm and eagerness to go to the next level, you will reap much more financial success. You will even tackle projects you have put off and make your dreams come true.

Psychologists have long understood that positive self-talk is helpful for people to engage in. That's why many psychologists have dedicated their careers to creating techniques to alter cognitive patterns and bring about more positive thinking. The results are proof that this approach works. Depression patients have managed to cure their conditions with positive self-talk. Olympic athletes and NBA players use self-talk to make big wins. People have even beat cancer just by changing the content of their self-monologues!

I promise that by the end of this book, you will know all of the techniques that will permanently change your self-talk for the better. If you put these techniques into action, then you will notice the rewards immediately. Your life will change into something greater than you ever imagined.

Don't wait. You have been unhappy for too long already. Since life is short, you should use the time you have now to make your dreams come true and enjoy being you. Read on to learn how to unlock your true potential with positive self-talk.

Chapter 1: Positive Self-Talk, The Negative Thought Eliminator

Positive self-talk is the core of happiness and high self-esteem. But negative self-talk is just the opposite. The purpose of positive self-talk is to regulate your inner dialogue to eliminate negative, self-defeating beliefs and unlock your true potential as a human being.

Negative self-talk is something that most people are naturally prone to due to a combination of environmental and genetic factors. It is basically a habit that can have extremely toxic effects on your overall attitude and life. Changing your self-talk is imperative for you to gain happiness and well-being.

First, learn about the problem and what it does to you, in order to gain motivation to eliminate negative thinking from your brain. The key to fixing any problem is understanding it thoroughly. Only then can you see the need to change and go about making those changes.

What Is Negative Self-Talk?

You know that narrative that runs in your head? "You can't do this, so why are you even trying?" "They must think I'm such an idiot." "She would never go out with me." "I need to get out of here because I'm way out of my element." Scolding yourself, making self-defeating statements to yourself, or telling yourself that life sucks are all examples of bad narrative.

That is negative self-talk in a nutshell.

Your self-talk is simply the way you talk to yourself inside of your head. The voice in your head that whispers wisdom can also whisper some pretty self-limiting and discouraging things. The voice may imitate your abusive parent, or your deepest insecurities, or your most denigrating boss, coach, or teacher.

The thing most people don't realize is that the self-talk you play in your own mind is taught, starting with your role models and parental figures in childhood [1]. It can also be altered in time by the people you surround yourself with and the experiences you go through in life. It is a fluid thing that changes with exposure to different environmental factors.

Therefore, self-talk can certainly be restructured to be more positive. Through repeated models in your environment, you learned how to think about yourself and life in a negative way. Now you can reframe that thinking in a more positive form with new models.

You might wonder why you should bother doing this. Well, the real question is, Why shouldn't you? Negative self-talk has been found to be the number one aggravator of issues like depression, anxiety, low self-esteem, and fear [2]. It has been found to create significant mental stress, which in turn is harmful to your physical health and impairing for your life performance [2]. Often, negative self-talk is comprised of several cognitive distortions, or improper ways of thinking that make life seem darker than it really is [2]. In other words, the way you are thinking is making you feel awful and it also may be causing or exacerbating any mental illnesses you may have.

This does not mean that you are to blame for your own suffering. You learned negative self-talk, and at the present moment, it is all you know. However, there is a fantastic solution that you can do yourself or with the help of a coach or therapist, so why not do it? By changing negative self-talk, you can start to correct the thinking patterns, or cognitive distortions, that underlie your problems.

Self-talk is how your mind harnesses language to regulate your behavior [3]. Think of how you might tell yourself, "Take a left up here" as you drive. Your arm follows that direction and turns the steering wheel left. When you are under social stress, such as at a job interview, that self-talk tells you what to do and say to win the job. Really, self-talk is quite necessary for your daily functioning.

Thus, it follows that negative self-talk instructs you to act negatively, which can have some detrimental effects on your overall life. Meanwhile, more positive self-talk has the opposite, and more desirable, effect.

We all have an inner critic that upholds us to higher standards. This critic is not always bad, provided that you look for solutions to your subpar work as opposed to beating yourself up mentally [3]. It is also not realistic to expect to be chipper and happy all of the time. Sometimes, dark moods and ugly thoughts will cloud your mind, obliterating the sunshine and rainbows. However, you don't need to live in a storm all of the time. Learning to change your negative self-talk can make you feel happier and more proactive, which in turn can exponentially improve your quality of life.

What Are The Causes Of Negative Self-Talk?

Negative self-talk has been recognized as a major factor in poor sports performance and low self-esteem since the 1990s, with some studies highlighting its significance even earlier. A focus of cognitive behavioral therapy, most psychologists and therapists understand that self-talk is critical your overall mental health and outlook on life.

However, the exact causes of negative self-talk are not as clear. There are many studies that have attempted to unlock the true causes. They have shed some light on possible reasons that people may engage in negative self-talk.

The first and foremost currently understood idea is

that self-talk is taught through environment. The influences that shape your mind when you are young, ranging from parents to school staff, can certainly affect the way you talk to yourself as you get older [4]. For instance, in a study of fifth-graders, many children in private school who received more praise and positive statements from their teachers, peers, and siblings had much higher self-esteem and higher rates of positive self-talk habits compared to public school students [4].

This study does not mean that you must go to a private school as a child to develop positive self-talk. Rather, it illustrates the effect that positive statements and praise can have on children and their self-esteem and self-talk. Children in private schools happen to receive more positive statements and praise, but a public school student who receives lots of encouragement can also develop high self-esteem and positive self-talk habits. It all starts in childhood.

Parents and teachers shape your mind when you are young; you look to them to model how the world is and how you should act [5]. If you are always hearing negative statements and criticism, you begin to believe that these words are true. As you grow older, you fear that other people will find out what a "failure" you are and confirm the negative statements that you heard throughout your life. Thus, you criticize yourself harshly, hang back in fear, and drive yourself crazy trying to be perfect in order to avoid hearing more hurtful statements [5].

But there may be a genetic predisposition to it, as well. If you have a genetic propensity for depression, anxiety, or other such mental disorders, then your mind is already "set up" for negative self-talk [6]. This hardly means that you can't change the behavior. It just means that you will tend to engage in self-talk despite having a positive upbringing and a good life, and this thinking habit is not a product of environment. With some habit-forming work, you can still address and change your self-talk to be more positive.

Negative life events can make negative self-talk appear [7]. A loss of a loved one is a major tragic event that can crumple your self-esteem and happiness. Rejections or difficult circumstances, like divorce, job termination, chronic illness, and bankruptcy, can also have this effect. Any traumatic experience, such as being the victim of a violent crime or abuse, witnessing a violent crime, surviving a catastrophe, or serving in a war, can further weaken your resolve to be happy, since you have seen the dark side of life. You may feel guilty for some perceived responsibility or fault in the event, which corrodes your self-esteem. You may have been manipulated by a person to believe that you deserved what has happened to you. No matter what happened, a bad experience or repeated bad experiences can muddy your positivity and make you take a gloomy outlook on life or even engage in self-loathing. Counseling and engaging in positive self-talk by choice can help you overcome the pain of these events.

Furthermore, social isolation can magnify negative self-talk [8]. Without positive influences to check your thinking, you don't have anyone to lift you up from dark or self-defeating thoughts. The sense that you are alone and that something must be wrong with you to keep you so isolated can further add to the gloom in your mind. You will notice that your mood can darken the more time you spend by yourself. Being social can certainly improve your self-talk.

The Consequences Of Negative Self-Talk

Now let's discuss why fixing negative self-talk is so essential. The consequences of negative self-talk are very real and very detrimental. Negative self-talk can corrode away your quality of life over time. Correcting it is imperative to maintaining happiness and good health.

Psychologists understand the fact that negative self-talk can harm you so well that they have dedicated a massive amount of time and research to developing cognitive behavioral therapies that rectify your narrative [9]. Various techniques have been established to help turn negative self-talk to positive self-talk. Athletes and businessmen are often taught these techniques because they are so effective in reversing negative self-talk and thus improving performance. These techniques are presented in the following pages, but first, learn why they are so important to use.

The voice in your head drags you down mentally, emotionally, spiritually, and physically. It negatively impacts your ability to be your best. As you repeatedly tell yourself that you aren't worthy or you can't do something, you begin to believe it. Then you waste potential because you don't even try. You hurt yourself repeatedly with these statements, which lowers your mood. You naturally fall into a pit of despair and self-loathing.

The first and foremost disastrous consequence of negative self-talk is low self-esteem. If you are constantly berating yourself mentally, you are not saying anything nice to build yourself up. The result is that you start to focus only on your flaws, which makes you hate yourself. As your self-esteem dwindles, so does your mental health. Low self-esteem has been linked to the gradual development of severe mental illness, ranging from depression to social anxiety to panic disorder [10]. One's self-esteem is considered the single most important aspect of mental and physical health, in fact [10].

This mental despair can spill into your physical health. There is a proven link between your health and your mental outlook. People with depression tend to have more physical health issues than those without depression [11]. In some cases, having a chronic illness can cause the despair and hopelessness that characterizes depression; but depression itself can also cause one to neglect his or her health and can lead to physical symptoms that cause health issues, such as overeating, ulcers caused by stress, sleep deprivation or oversleeping, lack of social activity, and lack of exercise [11].

Negative self-talk can also lead to sleep deprivation. As you stay up all night ruminating on what a bad person you are and how much you have ruined your life, you generate a massive amount of stress [2]. Depression tends to alter your melatonin production and increases cortisol production, which can keep you up at night [11]. Then your body is not able to heal from regular illnesses or injuries. You can experience weight gain, which comes with its own host of health problems. Furthermore, your concentration and mental clarity suffer, affecting your performance at work and in life in general. You can experience irritability and impulsive decision-making.

Not to mention how your social life will change for

the worse. If you are always down in the dumps, people don't think that you are fun to be around. You may also neglect or avoid social functions because you are scared of being criticized. As you neglect your social life, you tend to withdraw into social isolation, which only worsens negative self-talk and depression [8].

As you can see, each of the problems caused by negative self-talk tends to also exacerbate negative self-talk. So, as you engage in negative self-talk, your mind enters a vicious spiral that only drags you down further. The only way to change your life around and see improvement is to cut down on negative self-talk.

Chapter 2: Turning Back To Positive Self-Talk

Previously we covered why negative self-talk is bad. But now let's focus a bit on why positive self-talk is so good. Decades of scientific research has led to the realization that positive self-talk has numerous benefits for your life.

Benefits Of Positive Self-Talk

Most research has pointed to great benefits from positive self-talk. After some contradictory results from a 1980 study that failed to show any difference between elite skiers' performance and self-talk, Raalte and some other researchers decided to conduct a study of their own regarding self-talk and its effects on dart players to settle the debate once and for all.

They found that dart players who practiced positive self-talk before a game played better [12]. They generally had more confidence and higher scores. Players who engaged in negative self-talk had the opposite results. This study is largely what fueled the major trend of encouraging athletes to use positive self-talk before a big competition.

Nevertheless, this doesn't just apply to athletes or dart players. Positive self-talk can ease anxiety and heighten performance in anyone. It is useful before any big event that you feel nervous about. Talking yourself up before a big test, a job interview, a presentation at work, or asking someone out on a date can be beneficial. It can lead to success and victory on your part.

Positive self-talk has been indicated in several benefits [13]. Mainly, this form of self-talk can reduce anxiety. People who are less anxious tend to be more confident and take more action in life. Thus, positive self-talk can make you bolder and readier to take on new opportunities. It can reduce anxious thoughts, panic attacks, and social anxiety as well.

It also enhances self-confidence [12]. This is because it increases your belief in yourself and your love for yourself. As you talk yourself up, you believe what you tell yourself. It is true that we tend to believe what we think. Therefore, positive self-talk can help you feel at one with yourself and reduce the doubt and lack of confidence that can be so debilitating. Furthermore, confidence has been indicated to be more attractive to other people, so being confident can make you more popular [13].

Being more popular has the effect of also growing your confidence even more. As people praise you and give you good feedback, you begin to believe it. You begin to adopt the attitude that you are a likable person. Earning the approval of others starts with positive self-talk. This can make relationships healthier and more possible.

Positive self-talk also increases performance and effort [12]. If you give yourself a boost with positive self-talk, you tend to try harder. This may be because you actually believe you can do it and you want to prove to yourself that you can be successful. It may also relate to increased confidence and decreased anxiety. To make the most out of an event or perform at your best, use positive self-talk for motivation.

Needless to say, if you use positive self-talk and stop negative thoughts in their tracks, you can rework your mind to eliminate negative self-talk over time. Then you will counter the negative, toxic effects of negative self-talk. Depression, anxiety, and stress can all disappear with the use of positive self-talk. Be sure to practice it regularly to make it a habit.

Raalte observed other studies and found that positive self-talk by itself is not that useful. This is because you can undercut positive thoughts with negative ones. The true success of positive self-talk comes when you actively restructure your mind to no longer entertain negative self-talk. Thought stopping and cognitive restructuring were found to be the best ways to accomplish this [12]. Cognitive or dialectic behavioral therapy can be useful in teaching yourself to practice positive self-talk all of the time.

The dart players did not get a jolt just from thinking, "I can play really well today!" The ones who succeeded usually practiced positive self-talk in their daily lives. This positive self-talk was a habit for them. Meanwhile, the negative self-talk players who did not play as well generally engaged in negative self-talk in their daily lives. Thus, to really reap the benefits of positive self-talk, you must work to make it a daily habit. Only then will it fuel the changes you wish to see in your demeanor and overall life.

What Positive Self-Talk Is Like

Positive self-talk is much like conversing with a best friend who is struggling with something. When you engage in negative self-talk, you harshly criticize and condemn yourself, beating yourself up needlessly. You hurt yourself and don't actually accomplish anything. If anything, you work yourself up so much that you become totally frozen and inactive. Depression, anxiety, and stress-related health problems are thus born.

Would you talk to a friend like this? Chances are, no. You would instead try to praise and comfort your friend to help him or her through the said issue. You would accept his or her faults and imperfections with compassion and try to help him or her feel better.

You won't believe how wonderful it feels to stop beating yourself up. As you enter a new mental outlook on life, you start to feel so much better. You stop driving daggers into your own heart and instead treat yourself with the love and tenderness you would treat your best friend with.

You Will Look Better

As you begin to engage in positive self-talk, it will show in how you carry yourself, how you look, and how you talk and act. You may even dress in a more flattering way to reflect your renewed sense of self-importance and greatness. Other people will notice. Big life changes can start happening pretty rapidly, as people begin to extend opportunities to you and invite you to try new things. Having a good social life is a positive and enriching factor in life itself.

Be ready for people to start smiling at you more. You will generate positivity and cheer, which makes people feel good around you. You will also smile a lot without realizing it, as a reflection of your internal happiness. Other people will respond in kind. The exchange of smiles will only add to your sense of positivity.

You Will Make More Friends

Also, be ready for an influx of friends and new

acquaintances. New and positive experiences will come your way as more people enter your life. When you engage in positive self-talk, you speak more positively and take more positive action. People like this and respond to it well. More people will want to spend time around you as you spread around your wonderful attitude.

You will also have the confidence to try new things. You might go to that swing class you always wanted to attend, but never did out of fear that you would look like a clown dancing. You might start attending some sort of group or join a social club. This puts you in contact with more potential friends and grows your network. You can beat social anxiety and work up the courage to go out by talking to yourself positively.

Above all, you will be your own best friend. Out of everyone you meet in life, you are the only one that you are guaranteed to live with for the rest of your life. Hence, if you make it easy and pleasant to live with yourself by taking care of yourself, you will be much happier. You will find that positive self-talk encourages you to like yourself more, take better care of yourself, and treat yourself as a priority. This will make you infinitely happier.

Better Health Comes With Positive Self-Talk

You will feel infinitely better, as you begin to practice positive self-talk. You will notice improvements to your health and your mental well-being as you defeat depression and its debilitating symptoms.

Healthier habits and a sense of accomplishment will also accompany positive self-talk. You no longer feel as stressed, so you won't want to pig out on chips in front of bad TV as much as anymore. You will welcome healthy habits because they make you feel good and your self-talk reminds you that you deserve to feel good.

You will also have fewer urges to engage in unhealthy behavior such as smoking, gambling, or impulse shopping. Often, these bad habits are the result of stress. The brief adrenaline rush that comes with a gambling spree can make you feel better for an instant. Then the reality of what you have just done sets in and you feel even worse. It is a vicious cycle that can drag on for years. Positive self-talk can eliminate the need for these vices.

The reduction in stress that positive self-talk brings can eliminate depression, anxiety, stress-related weight gain, and insomnia. Your mind will be at ease, as well as your body. Say good-bye to frustrating symptoms and bad habits as you enter a new phase of true well-being.

Finances Will Improve

Be prepared for an uptick in your financial success. As you believe in yourself suddenly, you will have the confidence to take on opportunities and make your career happen. The bold career moves that you avoided before because you felt you weren't capable of handling them are now suddenly possible.

With negative self-talk, you might shy away from a lucrative business opportunity. "How can I possibly do that? It's too [insert self-defeating excuse] or I'm too [insert self-insult]." You perpetuate the idea that you can't achieve things. But when you switch that narrative, you start to see that things really are possible. You take charge and do things you never thought possible. Positive self-talk breaks down the barriers that are holding you back.

You might gain the confidence necessary to leave your job and shoot for that dream job or open your own business. Or you might use that new surge of confidence to start a new hobby and make some new friends. Either way, you will welcome and feel ready for new challenges and new opportunities.

Confidence will also increase your problem-solving abilities and your effort. You might perform better at work and bring home a pay raise or bigger commissions. Talk yourself up before you have to do something at work, and see how you perform more awesomely.

You Will Create A Positive Self-Talk Environment

The environment you live in drastically affects your ability to engage in self-talk. If you live in a negative environment, you are always inclined to think negatively. That can spread to your own self-image and treatment of yourself.

Positive self-talk can lead you to love yourself. As a result, you will no longer appreciate people or situations that hurt you. You will start to set up boundaries, defend yourself, and say no when you need to. You will no longer feel a desire to engage with hurtful or negative people who bring you down.

To facilitate positive self-talk, a positive environment

is ideal. You want to cut out toxic people and leave a stressful job where your horrible boss calls you names in front of the office. When someone hurts you, stage a healthy confrontation and ask the person to make amends.

Also, do what makes you happy. The happier you are, the more likely you are to engage in positive self-talk. Then positive self-talk will cause you to want to do things you enjoy. It's a self-sustaining cycle.

You Will Be Able To Create A Positive Self-Talk Environment For Others

Often, entire demographics can be hurt by negative self-talk. Kids growing up in a disenfranchised and impoverished area will often hear how life is unfair and the world is turned against them from their families. They grow up believing this and don't try because they think there is no use. A few manage to turn this self-talk around and enjoy considerable success, however. You hear stories every day about kids who grew up in the "ghetto" but went on to have amazing careers. Oprah Winfrey is a shining example.

Positive self-talk is important for teachers and parents to show their students [2]. Significant others should also show this to their partners. By modeling positive self-talk, you can create a habit in your child. Speak to your child nicely. Use constructive criticism. For instance, when your child does something wrong, you can gently tell him or her how to do it instead of yelling, "You always mess things up!"

Furthermore, you can set a model by always speaking to yourself and about yourself nicely. You are not setting a good model by berating yourself when you get into a car accident. Saying things like, "I'm so stupid" or "I always mess things up" teach your children to say this to themselves as well. Being kind to yourself, encouraging yourself, and refusing to talk badly about yourself denotes a massive amount of self-respect and self-love. Children will learn from this model and act the same way themselves.

An environment created around positive self-talk is warm and encouraging. You compliment people and tell them what they do best. You highlight their strengths and talents. You also do this to yourself, and you receive ample praise and encouragement back.

Think of a good home, where loving parents dote on their children. You don't hear a lot of cussing, name calling, or berating in this environment.

Think of a sports team, where all of the members build each other up. After a game, you hear the team members congratulate each other. They may offer suggestions for improvements, but they don't tear each other down or scream at each other. They also don't stand there criticizing themselves.

These are examples of positive environments. Focus on building such environments to influence those around you. In turn, you will influence yourself to take on this new approach to self-talk. Always set a model for others and you will receive benefits too.

By setting a model, you not only spread the habit of positive self-talk to children or other people around you, but you also have a reason to engage in positive self-talk. This can make the habit easier to develop because you have a good source of motivation.

How To Initiate Change

Now you see clearly how positive self-talk is the greatest invention since sliced bread! But that's not enough to make you change. There more to it, which you will learn in this book.

Change is not easy for anyone. People tend to settle into habits, including bad ones, and then encounter difficulties changing them because they are comfortable. Even if your thinking habits cause you considerable suffering, you are still comfortable engaging in these habits because you have done so for a long time [14].

The science of habit-formation indicates that habits are formed in one of two ways: System 1 or System 2 [14]. System 2, the most common *and* unsuccessful form of habit change, involves hearing "You need to change your negative thinking because it's bad for you!" You imagine how much better your life is going to be as long as you change, and then you decide to change and put all of your energy behind it. When you don't see results immediately, your motivation and attention wane, making you lose sight of your goals and let your new positive thinking habits fall to the wayside. You try to force a new habit and it just doesn't work.

The truth is that changing a habit takes a lot of action

and correction. Habits are automatic responses to stimulus [14]. Your brain saves time by automating its response so that you don't have to spend too much thinking, "What should I do now?" To correct your thinking, you must recognize your automatic habit of thinking negatively and then retrain your brain to automate positive thinking instead.

To successfully shape new habits, you must engage in a System 1 habit formation plan, which automates habits. This basically involves repeating a habit every day for 66 days without scanning too hard for results. At that point, automation takes over and you don't have to keep up the rigorous work [14]. Abandon the pressure of System 2 and simply use a reminder to engage in your habit once a day, 66 days in a row, and then your brain takes over for you. The results sneak up on you.

Another important aspect of System 1 habit formation is making the change easy, so you don't have to put in as much effort [14]. Work around your schedule. Write in your thought journal at a convenient moment for you, such as before bed, to take the stress out of clearing a patch in your schedule and dredging up the motivation to work on your habit.

Also, find a contextual clue to trigger your automatic reaction, so your brain never forgets to trigger its habitual response. Most of us wash our hands (habit) after using the bathroom (contextual clue). To find a contextual clue relevant to thinking, determine times when you are especially hard on yourself. This might be when you reflect on the day as you lie in bed, or when you submit a project to your boss at work, or when you have a confrontation. These times become your contextual cues. When the cue happens, you then know to activate your new positive self-talk habit to override the inevitable negative self-talk habit. Basically, you don't have to remind yourself to work on your self-talk anymore because you have chosen key times when you must work on it. Working on positive self-talk every time you get the cue and negative self-talk starts running in your head makes it an automatic habit with time.

How To Start Using System 1

The first step is to realize that you have a problem with negative self-talk. You have probably already completed this step since you are reading this book. The next step is to define the problem in simple words that your brain can clearly understand: "I use negative self-talk which damages my self-esteem and leads to other life problems." Write that statement down to cement it in your brain.

From there, you can start identifying the moments you have negative self-talk. In a journal, document the moments that you think negatively and the words you say to yourself. You might not be able to catch every single negative thought, but you can catch the main big ones.

Now, decide on helpful replacement thoughts. These are positive thoughts that should take the place of negative ones in your mind. For instance, if you forgot to buy bread on a grocery store run, your habit may be to tell yourself, "I forgot the bread! I'm such an idiot. I forget everything." A more helpful positive thought is something like, "Oops, I forgot the bread. It's OK because everyone forgets things now and then. I had better go back to get more bread."

The thoughts that kick you down a notch and make you feel bad need to go. For each of these thoughts, there is a subsequent positive one that you can use instead to uplift yourself and find a solution to a problem in your life. Find the contextual cues when your ugly thoughts start running amok in your mind, and then work on thinking about the replacement thoughts, even writing them down or reciting them out loud.

Also, take a moment to reflect on your motivation each day. Write down a statement about why you want to change your thinking. This helps cement System 1 habit formation by keeping you invested in your new endeavor.

As you begin to plan how to talk to yourself, you are in a good place to start implementing the techniques in the next chapter. You already know the problem and how you want to change. Now you just need to know the methods and how to build motivation.

Chapter 3: The Secrets To Positive Self-Talk

To begin using positive self-talk and eradicating negative self-talk, there are several things you can do. These activities will change your thinking and your approach to situations in life. With time and practice, they become habitual routine, so you start to use positive self-talk regularly.

In addition, using positive self-talk and different methods to attain that attitude will show you how great it can be. Thus, you feel more motivated to use it more often. Experience can be an excellent motivator. These techniques help you change your thinking so that you see quick results and experience rapid relief. Then, you can start to implement them in your daily life when you realize how wonderful they are for your mental and physical health.

Self-Distance

It is possible to put distance between yourself and a situation to think about it objectively [3]. Think of how someone else might see you. If you think, "Another person would see me as an abject failure," then think of how you could change your behavior so that someone would see you as a success.

Self-distance is a great way to remove the emotion from a thought process and make a logical decision that is ideal for your situation [3]. It can also help you determine the necessary actions to actually affect change in your life. Just talking to yourself positively is a helpful action, but it's not enough to make a real difference. The difference starts when you use self-talk to drive positive action and positive decisions in your life.

By putting self-distance in place, you can focus more on finding a solution to a problem that is troubling you. When you are looking at life from inside of your own lens, you only see the limitations and hurdles that you have erected around yourself. It is thus easy to get lost in despair and give up. By removing these lenses and thinking, "What is best for this person?", as if evaluating yourself from someone else's standpoint, it becomes more obvious what you must do. Then you can objectively address the limitations and hurdles, removing them without dwelling on the pain and frustration they cause you.

I'll never forget the day I decided to go back to college. For years, I had worked dead-end jobs and thought, "I can't possibly afford to go back to college." I would read cool job postings, then see the requirement for a bachelor's or higher and abandon the posting, thinking, "Good jobs just aren't for me." One day, I thought, "I obviously want to go to college and I need to. The best decision, to make me a person that I'm proud of, is to go back. So, let's see how to make this possible." From there, I made a series of good decisions that helped me get back on track: I sought the help of an academic advisor to align myself with my desired degree, I looked into financial aid, I took a few community college classes to prepare for my degree at my state university, and I ultimately graduated into a new life.

Another example is Lebron James [3]. When choosing between staying with his small-market team for nostalgic reasons or moving to a larger team which scared him, he was torn by emotion which removed his ability to reason. Then he decided to remove the emotion from the equation by putting self-distance in place and asking himself, "What would make Lebron James happy?" The answer thus became clear to him: Go to the larger team. Now he is a famous basketball player featured in the Basketball Hall of Fame. He probably never would have made it so far had he not made this huge life decision using self-distance.

Utilize Self-Talk

At times, negative self-talk can be a useful tool for

elevating yourself to a better position or for driving better performance. For instance, if you perform some sloppy work and you know it, you can direct yourself to improve the work into something great that you are proud of.

Being able to criticize yourself can be useful, as long as you use that criticism to better yourself. All humans have a built-in self-critic. This self-critic regulates your behavior through language [3]. The problem lies in letting this self-critic tell you that you can't do something or you are not good enough.

There is nothing wrong with listening to your self-critic, as long as you use it as a motivational tool to make improvements. Always focus on solutions to the flaws you see in your performance. You don't want to just dwell on the fact that you are imperfect, as that doesn't help anything or anyone at all. Instead, think, "I don't like what I just did. How can I make it better? How can I get the results I want?"

It is unrealistic to expect to be happy all of the time, or to expect yourself to always be perfect. Accepting the fact that you are imperfect opens your eyes to ways to improve upon your imperfections for better outcomes. Noticing that something is wrong in your work, your marriage, your friendship, your habits, or your personality enables you to make beneficial changes. Being blind to problems in life only prevents you from handling them.

Therefore, negative self-talk is not always the enemy. Allow this self-talk to arise at times and listen to it. Harness the insight you gain from it by chasing every negative thought with, "Is this something I really need to address?" If the self-talk is pointing out a very real problem that can decline the quality of your life in some way, then you should address it.

The next thought to chase the first one with is, "How can I go about fixing this?" When you make negative self-talk a source of inspiration for recognizing and solving a problem, it immediately becomes a very positive tool in your self-toolbox.

Let's say you are used to beating yourself up for being fat. That is not good because you are only hurting your mental health and causing stress with these thoughts. The stress can lead to you eating more as a source of comfort, so you only gain more weight. To beat out of this cycle, listen to yourself the next time you think bitterly, "I'm such a whale." Then, think, "I hate being a whale because of how people look at me and how I am hurting my health. My quality of life is suffering because of my weight." From there, ask yourself, "What can I do about my weight to stop feeling so bad about myself and hurting myself? How can I fix my weight-related problems?" Use the pain you feel as being overweight to drive your desire to lose it and get healthy and fit.

"Fat talk" is a perfect example of harmful negative

self-talk at play. People who hear fat talk in the media or from friends internalize it and begin to think that it is true. They then suffer from a sharp decline in body image satisfaction, which can lead to depression, overeating, or eating disorders [15]. Yet people who enjoyed successful weight loss were able to use fat talk to their advantage. They let the pain and dissatisfaction motivate them to lose weight.

Hence, there is no reason to beat yourself up if you still use negative self-talk from time to time. Talking to yourself negatively because you are talking to yourself negatively is pretty silly. Instead, use this habit constructively. Gain some good out of it. Then, you will reap more benefits than if you simply try to force yourself to be positive all of the time.

Importance Of Repeating

In order to make positive self-talk a habit, you must make non-negativity a habit. The best way to do this is to use repetition [14]. Repetition will drill messages into your head and provide you with a clear idea of what you need to do.

To start using positive self-talk, you must repeat positive messages. You can do this after you think a negative thought by forcing yourself to think a positive one. Chase negative thoughts with positive ones. Another way is to think positively at certain times throughout the day, repeating mantras by rote. Read on to the part about mantras to learn how to do this.

Here's an example. You hit the curb. Your impulse in this stressful moment is to think, "You dummy!" You may yell it out loud or yell it in your head, but the negative message is obvious and hateful toward yourself. Then you chase that thought with another one: "I need to pay more attention. I'm actually a good driver."

Doing this often can drill the habit of positive self-talk

into your head and show you how to talk to yourself more positively. Try a little positive self-talk every day, even if you have to force it, and you will notice it becomes easier and easier. Pretty soon, you won't need to force it anymore.

Here is why repetition works. Many people think that habits are formed by reward. If you work out and see how good you feel after, you are more likely to keep working out. But anyone who has struggled with getting in enough gym time understands that habit formation doesn't work like that. A study suggests that habits are formed through repetition, *not* reward [16].

This study compared people who strove to form habits by receiving rewards and those who formed habits through repetition. Guess who actually formed habits? The ones who used repetition [16]. The result is clear, that repetition will rewire your brain to be more positive than simply focusing on the rewards of thinking positively.

People don't form habits based on the outcomes of their behavior. This is why the horrible habit of negative self-talk sticks, because your brain doesn't focus on the negative outcomes. This is why people get "addicted" to things despite outrageously bad outcomes – they don't learn from outcomes, but rather from the actions they have already performed.

Rather, the brain builds habits based on recently performed actions. So, to change your habits, you must perform the actions of positive self-talk [16]. Only then will your brain start to make positive self-talk a habit. It won't care about how great positive self-talk is or how you really should do it; the brain is somehow impervious to learning by outcomes, as much as we would like to think otherwise.

But how much repetition is necessary? As discussed under System 1, it can take 66 days to form a habit.

Practicing positive thinking and positive self-talk in some manner for 66 days should provide sufficient repetition to make the habit stick.

Using these study results constructively, you now know to perform positive self-talk every day for 66 days. But you should also drive home the habit of stopping negative thoughts or using negative thoughts constructively. That will also become a good habit that reinforces your new habit of positive self-talk. Positive self-talk can only occur in a vacuum where negative self-talk does not exist. Learning how to stop negative self-talk *and* engage in positive self-talk is a two-fold habit formation process that can be accomplished through rote.

The Reprogramming Process

Computers were modeled after the actual human brain. Thus, the brain works a lot like a computer and you have more control over it than you think. It is actually possible to reprogram your mind, just as you would reprogram software or install a whole new operating system on your computer.

Reprogramming is the simple act of taking your thoughts and directing them to behave differently. Gain a clear idea of what you want your new mind to be like. Think about how you want to use more positive self-talk in your thinking. Then, capture your negative thoughts and make them do what you want.

Ultimately, this process lets you gain victory over the most elusive and rebellious part of your body: your mind. You might think, "I have all sorts of renegade thoughts! I can't control what I'm thinking! What are you talking about, taking my thoughts captive and changing them?" But this process is more than possible. Reprogramming is a step-by-step process that may take some time to become a habit.

Reprogramming is possible because of neuroplasticity [17]. This is your brain's ability to learn things and then form new neural pathways to accommodate the new information and a subsequent appropriate reaction. For instance, you were probably a naïve youth once, and then you got your heart broken for the first time. Your brain never knew betrayal and heartbreak of the romantic sort before, so when it encountered it, it reprogramed itself to accommodate trust issues and a fear of abandonment in an effort to avoid being hurt again. Fortunately, just as the brain can reprogram itself negatively, it can also reprogram itself more positively to get over such learning behaviors as trust issues or, of course, negative self-talk.

Dr. John Demartini is a leader in mental reprogramming using neuroplasticity. He uses a technique where he neutralizes the fear and aggression of the amygdala by having someone think about the good that comes from a bad situation [17]. This makes the brain start to think differently and form new neural pathways in response to the situation that causes it so much pain.

For instance, maybe your parent abandoned you when you were little and you now have a propensity for negative self-talk, rooted in the belief that you are not good enough which is why your parent left. By thinking about that horrible experience made you a strong person more than capable of surviving on his or her own, you start to reprogram your thoughts about the abandonment. You make your brain stop resorting to its old path of thought: "I am not good enough." You instead think, "I am a strong person." The result is that you eliminate a lot of dark thoughts about yourself and a lot of negative self-talk just be reframing your perspective on the situation.

Tony Robbins also offers a method of reprogramming that combines physical movement with new feelings [18]. Called priming, Robbins suggests this method to prime your brain to feel something different. When you are feeling negative, sit in a chair, and close your eyes. Raise your fists and then breathe out through your nose, lowering your fists. Do this thirty times.

Focusing on this behavior raises your heart rate while clearing your head. Then you feel neutral. You are able to flood yourself with love and gratitude, which can make your brain take a different neural route than its usual one of anger, bitterness, or anxiety.

Robbins recommends starting the day with this so that you are able to neutralize emotions and then make them positive throughout the next twenty-four hours. But you can also use priming whenever you feel the negative self-talk build up to a fever pitch in your mind. Either way, you can reprogram your mind's response to things using priming.

Furthermore, affirmations and visualizations are incredibly effective methods of reprogramming. I cover them shortly. Pairing them with these methods when you start to think negatively will have a similar effect on your thinking.

When the negative self-talk starts, actively try to

reprogram your mind by priming yourself with Robbins' method. As you feel better after, you can start to look at your situation differently by asking a series of questions that lead to positive thinking, through Demartini's method. The two methods combined can have a really positive effect on your overall thinking. They can train your brain to focus on the positive and to stop harboring negative emotion.

When you think about an upsetting memory, you are really remembering the last time you remembered it. Usually, the last time you remembered it, you felt negative. But once you use one or both of these reprogramming methods, you think about it positively for once. The next time the memory comes up, you thus remember it in the positive way you did during the reprogramming session. This creates a habit and completely restructures how your brain handles the memory.

Sometimes, people want to hold onto anger. Anger

fuels them more than sadness and feels more proactive, even though it really is not. Thus, it may be hard for you to want to reprogram your brain. It feels better to cling to grudges or "comfortable" negative thinking.

You may also find it difficult to face a memory or find anything good about something bad that happened to you. As long as you attempt it, you can begin the reprogramming process that can eradicate the negative views you have about yourself based on past abuse, abandonment, or trauma. Chances are, your negative self-talk is rooted in some negative self-belief fueled by an unkind memory, such as a parents' criticism or some horrible event from your past.

If you find it too difficult to do this on your own, therapy can help. A hypnotherapist or psychologist who specializes in EMDR can reprogram your brain through questions, affirmations, and repetitive movements. They can help you feel less alone as you revisit extremely troubling traumas. They can also point out a silver lining if you can't see one yourself. Having a trained outside perspective when dealing with brain reprogramming can be extremely helpful.

Importance Of Visualization

Neurolinguistic programming, or NLP, teaches you to change your modality to reprogram your own brain [19]. Your modality is simply how you see and understand the world inside your mind. People operate on different modalities, but all modalities are based on the same principle: They are a way for your brain to process the information it takes in from the world in a simplified way using one of the main senses: sight, sound, taste, smell, or touch [19]. Most people use sight or sound as their primary modality [19].

Negative self-talk is an example of an auditory modality. You are processing the world around you and instructing yourself how to respond to life events or situations with verbal cues. You are "hearing" the voice inside your head, or in other words, you are hearing yourself think.

To use visualizations to change negative self-talk, you must change your auditory modality to a visual one. This makes the negative self-talk irrelevant. It can be pretty difficult to scold yourself or call yourself an idiot with an image. If you do, the image will probably be pretty silly and make you laugh, which lessens the negativity of the situation.

Processing the world in a more visual way can help you step back. It can help you "see" things more clearly. But mostly, it just removes all of the verbal garbage that you are abusing yourself with. Instead of focusing on calling yourself a dummy or a failure, you can focus on how the situation looks right now and how you want it to look.

Furthermore, visualizations can act as distractions.

You essentially remove yourself from the equation as you focus your energy on imagining some sort of complex image. Guided meditations help you relax by channeling your energy into visualizing a peaceful forest, for instance. By using a visualization technique, you can stop thinking about your negative self-image and distract yourself to something more pleasing. Then, you can return to problem-solving mode in a more relaxed mood, and you can approach finding a solution without abusing yourself.

A powerful visualization will first feature something that calms you down. Perhaps imagine a nice beach setting or a forest where you can only hear the wind in the leaves and the birds chirping. As you settle your nerves, you can move on to the next part.

The next part must feature your problem or your feelings. You must visualize them in a lifelike form. For instance, maybe you are beating yourself up for displeasing your boss, who always calls you a useless idiot. You can reduce your boss to a yammering cartoon to make him appear both smaller and less intimidating than you are making him out to be.

The third part involves visualizing how you vanquish this problem. This part teaches your brain that your problems are surmountable. Something can be done, and you can do it. This gives your brain confidence to tackle the problem in real life.

The final part involves picturing yourself as the victor. You want to create an image of yourself that helps you feel good. Being that victorious knight in shining armor, or that beautiful princess who just fought off an army, can make you feel better about yourself. It can also show your brain how you *could* be if you handled your problem with an effective solution.

Visualizations work in these four parts because they illustrate something to your brain. They send an actual message that alters your brain's perception of reality. As you sit ruminating on a problem and speaking to yourself vulgarly, you are engaging in a limited aspect, where your brain magnifies the problem. The visualization shows your brain that it is more than possible to view this problem differently, to stop making it so huge, and to deal with it effectively so that you emerge victoriously.

Let's look at the actual science behind visualizations. How do they actually work? Several studies have shown that the brain processes visualizations, or imagined scenarios, the exact same way as real scenarios [20]. Hence, there is really no difference between what you actually see and what you imagine. Your brain treats both as reality and remembers both. So when you visualize something in relation to a real-life troubling situation, your brain responds to the visualization like it's really happening.

It has been found that visualizing a routine is the

same as practicing it in real life [20]. Thus, if you have a big dance recital coming up, you can visualize it when you're not practicing and that just helps you practice yet more. The same logic applies to restructuring your self-talk. If you visualize handling your problems in the right way and talking to yourself nicely, it is just as effective as doing it in real life. Your brain considers it valuable practice and absorbs it, making your visualized work part of its reality.

When you start to engage in negative self-talk, take a moment to visualize something that increases your positivity. That way, your brain is focused on a more positive emotion or action. That helps you speak to yourself more kindly. There are many visualization methods that you can employ, but you must ensure that they reframe you in a more positive light. The result is that you reprogram your brain to view you in a more positive light. That eliminates unpleasant self-talk.

Imagine that you feel bad after your boss chews you out. As you sit at your desk, you start to beat yourself up and tell yourself the things your boss just said. You start to believe the worst about yourself. Then you take a step back and visualize yourself in a better light, as the conqueror of your life. When you come back to reality, you believe that you are better than what your boss said, and you are full of confidence to prove it to your boss.

How Do You Visualize?

Your brain is your kingdom. You can do anything you want to do with your visualizations. Find something that works for you by imagining different scenarios that involve the four parts discussed above: relaxing pleasantly, encountering your problems in a smaller form, vanquishing your problems, and emerging as the victor. You may also download a guided visualization app or look one up online and follow it. Whatever brings you relief, quiets the negative self-talk, and encourages you to move forward is great.

For example, I will share what I like to visualize.

1. I picture myself in a plain or meadow at dusk, wearing armor and wielding a magical butterfly sword. This image is beautiful and powerful and it relaxes me.

2. I start to walk through the meadow, taking in how beautiful it is. I take in the setting sun and the wildflowers. Maybe I see a rainbow. I can feel the ground under my feet as I walk, and I can smell the fresh air. This relaxes me yet more as I stop focusing on my problems and instead focus on the construction of a beautiful fantasy world.

1.

3. I then gather up my imaginary army of squirrels, foxes, and rainbow

zebras that make me feel safe. I now have allies and I am not alone in the world. That is a comforting thought.

2.

4. Next, I encounter my thoughts. I visualize the terrible thoughts as having physical forms. They take the shapes of ugly trolls, warty dwarves, and evil serpents. Each thing that is bringing me down gets an image that is equivalent to its severity and magnitude in my life.

3.

5. I take my army and go in for the kill. With my sword, I slash down my enemies and then they disappear with a satisfying popping sound. I also picture my army fighting with me, taking out enemies that are too strong for me. No one enemy is left standing.

4.

6. I hold up my sword, which is dripping with blood, and yell, "I am the victor!" I imagine the sunset lighting up my armor, which doesn't even have a dent. The wind streams my hair behind me as I raise my chest. I feel truly strong and wonderful in this visualization.

5.

Here is another one I like to use when I am dealing with hurtful things I say to myself. I imagine what I have to say to myself, as if someone else is saying it to me, and I let it hurt me. I acknowledge the pain as a stab wound. Then I picture the person's voice turning into a cartoon voice that makes me laugh. I picture it getting sillier and sillier, and quieter and quieter, until it fades away. The stab wound feeling is now gone. The words I have said to myself are now gone too, and they don't mean anything. They are just words. I can now move on.

I may also visualize a person who has hurt me. I

visualize the person's face in front of me in color. I let the person speak, hearing their words in my mind. Then I mute the picture, as if it were a TV. I switch it to black and white. I turn it into a black and white cartoon or slapstick, like something from the 1950s, so that it seems silly. This helps me take it less seriously. After that, I start shrinking the frame of the TV picture until it is so small that I can't see it. Now, this person is gone; I can't see or hear what he or she said. And I have not allowed myself to engage in belittling self-talk in relation to the person's words. I certainly didn't internalize their words as the truth about myself. They are just a little voice that has disappeared from my mind and they are no longer relevant!

When I am stressed, I tend to use more negative self-talk. I defeat myself by thinking that I can't handle the situation at hand because I'm too overwhelmed. That is when I visualize myself walking along a peaceful beach, listening to the waves lapping at my feet, hearing the seagulls spiraling over my head. As a result, I instantly feel more serene. My brain believes the stress is gone and stops reacting to it. When I come back to reality, I am in a better place to handle my business because I no longer feel stressed.

Visualizations also work well with traumatic memories. When you start to have a flashback to a bad memory, you can take control of it. Tell yourself, "I want it to end differently now." Visualize a totally different set of events and outcome. Imagine what you could have done differently and do it in your mind. Emphasize your sense of righteousness and victory at the end. This helps you reprogram the memory, so that it no longer troubles you as much. It makes your brain believe that you are not weak and powerless and you can do something about the events that hurt or trouble you.

You can download a guided meditation or watch one on Youtube. You can also invent your own visualizations. The key is to force yourself into a new emotional state that gets rid of the trouble and torment of whatever you are dealing with. From that positive space, you can build yourself up. Your brain learns from this as if it's real life and takes a new approach to situations as a result.

The Power Of Mantras

The power of reciting mantras to yourself cannot be understated. Truthfully, mantras are a great way to teach your brain something useful. By repeating a sound or Sanskrit phrase over and over, you make its message clear to yourself. Your brain absorbs it and pays attention to it.

People use mantras to drive life change. The massive power of mantras has been realized and recognized by many. That's why mantras are a go-to method for many people who are trying to change themselves. They are also a cornerstone in Buddhist meditation, which says something about their ability to change the mind.

The same science that lies behind repetition and visualization also lies behind mantras. Mantras use an auditory modality because you are speaking to yourself. They use repetition to make your brain remember and understand their message. Finally, they use the power of visualization to make your brain adopt them as fact.

A mantra is something short and easy to remember. The catchier or snappier it is, the more your brain will retain it. Think of how you easily remember little commercial slogans or jingles and apply that to your mantras. A simple sentence or sentence fragment is ideal; your brain will be less likely to retain a huge, flowery sentence. You may also use a basic sound that intones a specific meaning for you, or a word in another language that captures the essence of what you are trying to say.

When you repeat the mantra, close your eyes and

really focus on what it means for you. Then repeat it over and over. Let the feeling it is supposed to bring you overtake your body.

That conditions your brain to associate the mantra with a particular state. When you use the mantra in the future, your brain automatically recalls the state it is supposed to be in. The association is strong but may need to be renewed. Be sure to set aside some time for meditation where you focus on the mantra and the feeling you want it to symbolize. That keeps the association strong and enduring.

An example of a mantra is the meditation "Om." When you say "Om," you immediately recall the feeling of being calm, collected, and centered in meditation. Even if you can't meditate and reach that particular feeling in a moment, you can still say "Om" and your brain makes you feel that way. This gives you power over yourself and your situation by letting you control your emotional state.

Find a mantra that means a lot to you. Then repeat it when you need it. You can make one up, or use a popular meditation mantra. You can even use a simple phrase in English or imagine an image, such as a lotus flower. Use the mantra a few times in meditation to condition your brain to it and then use it when you need it throughout the hustle and bustle of your daily life.

Positive Affirmations

Positive affirmations work in the same way as mantras. In fact, they are practically the same thing. The main difference is that mantras can simply be sounds you use to gain a certain feeling, while affirmations are statements that you make as truth. As you recite affirmations to yourself, you come to believe them.

Positive affirmations are auditory modalities when

you speak them out loud to yourself. They can become visual if you write them or use them in a picture. You can find thousands of positive affirmations online, complete with pictures that reinforce their power.

As you say an affirmation, you start to believe it with repetition. However, you also invoke a feeling with it. It works just like a mantra in this way.

You can have more than one affirmation that you use throughout the day, but one affirmation that drives home the thinking you really want to work on the most is sufficient. Designate an affirmation for each negative self-talk-triggering situation you struggle with. Also, find one that illustrates the main problem you struggle with each day, such as a self-defeating belief or fear. Recite your main affirmation several times a day. Recite the other affirmations when the situation arises that makes them applicable. Recite them at least three times to make them stick in your brain.

To adopt both visual and auditory modalities and cement affirmations more thoroughly in your brain, you can write them down and place them somewhere that you see often. A Post-It note on your laptop with your favorite affirmation is a great idea. I have my computer background set to a revolving series of positive affirmation quotes that I have found online. Then, read the affirmation and repeat it a few times throughout the day. The use of two modalities makes your brain actually believe the affirmation.

One critical aspect of affirmations is to leave out negative words like "not." Don't say something like, "I'm not a bad person." This affirmation doesn't work because it implies negativity and shifts your focus onto the term *bad person*. It can have its opposite intended effect. Instead, use positive language. "I am a good person" is better than "I'm not a bad person." Frame your affirmations to always say the best about yourself. Leave out the phrases and images that are not so friendly.

One example of a positive affirmation might be: "I am a good person." You can repeat this over and over until you believe it. This unearths the belief lying underneath your negative self-talk that you are not a good person.

Or you could say something like, "I got this." I hear a lot of people tell themselves this short, simple phrase before a big task or overwhelming project. The beauty of it is that it works. It undermines the belief that you can't do something. It assures you that you will tackle whatever big obstacle or undertaking lies before you.

"Not my circus, not my monkeys" is an affirmation I use a lot. I tend to internalize what people say to me, letting their words define my reality and self-image. The thing is, what other people think of me does not define me. I realize this fact, but my brain has the habit of forgetting it. So, I remind myself of this fact by reciting this little mantra a few times. It tells my brain to let what someone says or does go, because that person is separate from me and his or her drama is not mine.

"Life is good. I have a lot," is another good one to intone gratitude. Many people have a habit of focusing on the bad in life and forgetting the blessings they do have. This can make you turn bitter and dissatisfied. To remind yourself that you have more than you lack, be sure to recite this affirmation more than once a day. Pair it with a gratitude journal, where you reflect on your day and write down three things you have or that you did well.

"I am beautiful, inside and out," is a great affirmation for people struggling with their physical image. It increases body satisfaction and inspires a sense of confidence. When you start to criticize your looks or internalize something mean someone said to you about your appearance, remind yourself of this fact by reciting this affirmation. You may also use this affirmation if you tend to believe that you are not a good person or you are at fault for everything wrong in others' lives.

"I am worthy" or "I deserve this" is a great affirmation. Many of us feel unworthy of the best, of success, or of our dreams. We find something fundamentally inadequate or flawed within ourselves and then use that to justify fear for going after what we want or accepting something wonderful from life. Instead of doing this, ease up on yourself. Say "I am worthy" and think of all of the things you have done to deserve the best in life.

"I am worth more than this" is a good affirmation for those who are tolerating subpar treatment from others. If your significant other or boss is tearing you down, for instance, you can think this. This affirmation helps you realize that you don't deserve to be abused and mistreated in any way. It gives you the strength to remove toxic people from your life and elevate yourself to a happy existence.

"I am strong" can help you in the face of defeating life circumstances. A lot of addicts like to use an affirmation like this when they feel as if they are about to crumble to cravings. You can use it if you feel scared or weak. It will convince your brain that you do have the strength to accomplish anything, from sobriety to handling a big stressful project at work. It also works for grief, as it reminds you that you will survive despite your devastating emotions.

You can find your own affirmations. Whatever gives you the feeling you need to get through a situation that normally hurts you will work. Affirmations are useful as long as you actually repeat them. With time, they become a comforting ritual that really reprograms your brain.

Fight Negative Thoughts with Thought Stopping

It is a paradigm of human nature that the more you try not to think about something, the more you think about it. If you have ever dieted, for instance, you will notice that you think more about food when you try not to.

The same goes for negative thinking. If you try to not think negative thoughts, you will think about them the same amount or even more. Then, you are still in the same boat. Dwelling on negative self-talk or beating yourself up for engaging in it is self-defeating.

Banishing negative thoughts is neither possible nor helpful. You simply start to overthink about negativity. Therefore, a better approach is to simply stop negative thoughts in their tracks, without dwelling on them too much. Don't give them any of the attention that they don't deserve.

Since you have engaged in negative self-talk for most

of your life, it is a habit. You can and will encounter negative self-talk and thoughts throughout your journey into reprograming your brain for positive self-talk. Handling this inevitability the right way will only broaden your success.

Here is the wrong way to handle these thoughts. When a negative thought enters your mind, your habit is to think something else negative. "There I go again, using that negative self-talk!" You begin to beat yourself up for using negative self-talk. That is not helpful at all.

Rather, acknowledge the thought calmly. Think, "That thought was negative. I'd rather not think like that. How can I reframe this more positively?" That immediately puts your mind on a more positive track, which invites further positivity.

Then stop the thought. Briefly and firmly tell it to stop. Don't entertain it anymore. Start to think something more positive.

Acknowledge thoughts instead of suppressing them or reprimanding yourself for thinking them. Take notice of them. Think about how they are present. Then tell them to stop and calmly think of something else. This is how you "capture" your thoughts and make them obey you. You don't use force; you use calm but deliberate halting and then redirection [21].

Thought stopping is a common practice in cognitive behavioral therapy [21]. CBT encourages you to sit down with a CBT journal (any journal will do) and write down the most common stressful thoughts you suffer from. These might range from "How can I pay all the bills this month?" to "How can I possibly get all this work done?" These thoughts all have a root in a negative self-belief, probably a belief that you are not good enough and not capable of great things.

Next, imagine the thought. Let it fill it with the dread

or panic it normally causes you. You know exactly how this thought makes you feel, because you think it often.

Stop the thought by shouting "Stop!" Then close your eyes and think it again. Again shout "Stop!" You will startle yourself out of the thought each time. You just successfully stopped it.

Practice this a few times. Then start whispering "Stop." See the thought become interrupted. Eventually, you can just imagine yourself saying "Stop" and it will work.

Once the thought has been stopped, your mind is empty. It will struggle to fill the emptiness, and will probably resort to another negative thought by habit. You can retrain it not to, though, by repeatedly thinking a more positive thought.

In the same journal you write the thoughts down in, write accompanying good thoughts. For example, if you think about how you can't make enough money to cover the bills, think, "I'll find a way or I'll cut bills."

Subsequent positive thoughts can't just be empty platitudes like "Everything will be OK." You must actually reassure yourself by finding a potential solution to a worry. Think about how you can solve a problem. Then you prove to yourself that your worries are groundless and that you are capable of achieving success despite the obstacles that you may face in life. This goes miles for boosting your confidence and your ability to believe in yourself.

Some worries are totally groundless, with no solution. If you constantly worry about getting cancer, for instance, there is little you can do about that besides attempting to live a healthy life. In this case, stop the thoughts and think instead about how healthy you are. "I don't have cancer!" is the ideal chaser to this negative thought.

When you start to berate yourself with negative self-talk, use the same technique. Acknowledge the thought and how awful it makes you feel. This thought has a root and wants to be expressed, so don't suppress it. Then tell the voice to stop. Next, think of something more positive. You might call yourself an idiot. Think about how bad you feel saying that to yourself, say stop in your head, and then think, "I made a mistake. I'm a very intelligent person." Doing this with repetition really helps you master your self-talk and learn to stop it before it runs amok in your head, destroying your self-esteem.

This same process can spill over into your interactions with others. IF you start to talk badly to someone, you can tell yourself to stop and speak more kindly. If someone speaks badly to you, you can tell them to stop and ask them to speak more gently.

Watch how it helps you redefine and strengthen your communication. What goes in your head tends to come out in your actions, so making your mind a more positive place can make your life more positive.

From now on, when a negative thought intrudes on your mind's peace, always use CBT to stop the thought by whispering "Stop." Then follow the thought up with a more positive one.

Mental Decluttering

Many people suffer what is called "monkey mind." This term comes from Siddhartha Buddha, who likened the mind to monkeys swinging from branch to branch. Your mind jumps around like a monkey, seemingly out of your control. Negative thoughts intrude, no matter how much you don't want them. Fear infiltrates your reasoning. A ton of distracting thoughts clutter your mind, causing you to get lost in them, basically paying more attention to the monkeys swinging around than to your actual work at hand.

A few habits tend to drive this monkey mind more than others. Here are the habits that you should avoid to de-clutter your mind and have more control over your thinking.

The first is procrastination. As you put things off, you tend to weaken your ability to succeed. You cause yourself guilt over your lack of productivity and you beat yourself up for not getting ahead in life. The true cause of procrastination is usually fear of failure. But realize that procrastination will cause you to fail far more than trying will. Actually put in some effort and you will see what is possible.

Generalizations are also harmful. They are a listed cognitive distortion in CBT, or in other words, a harmful thought habit that distorts your perception of reality in a bad way [22]. This is where you think "That man hurt me, so all men are bad." Or you think, "I didn't get that job at a design studio so I must be a horrible designer and I won't get any jobs in this field." You take one instance and apply it to every other possibility in life.

Instead of generalizing, recognize that each person and each situation is different. Even if you have tried to get jobs at many studios with poor results, there is always that one that may accept you. Even if you have dated many horrible men, you are learning from them and one day you will be ready for the right man. Don't apply one, or even several, experiences to life in general. Keep trying and addressing each opportunity or situation as something different.

Evaluations are another cognitive distortion where you compare yourself to others, often unfairly [22]. This causes feelings of jealousy and inadequacy that prevent you from ever enjoying your life or feeling proud of who you are. You might evaluate yourself by thinking how someone you know is so much more accomplished at your age.

The truth is, everyone is different and you can't make an evaluation fairly. Your circumstances have led you to where you are. You don't have to be like your accomplished friend. Furthermore, you might not realize what your friend lacks that you have. Your friend's life may look wonderful on the outside, but it may not be so perfect on the inside. You can't make an evaluation because you will never have all of the facts.

Learn to accept yourself for who you are, instead. If you feel that you are lacking something that somebody else has, work for it. But don't let these feelings of lack create a sense of inadequacy within yourself. Otherwise, you will continually feel defeated and useless or unaccomplished.

Presuppositions, or assumptions, are also harmful because they cause you to operate on a lack of true knowledge. You may assume that someone hates you because he looked at you angrily one day. You don't realize that he was thinking about his bad day and didn't mean to look at you that way. Always get the full facts before you make a decision. Don't assume that you know how other people think or feel about you, and don't assume that you know all about a situation. Get the full facts before you start beating yourself up or making reckless decisions.

Also, avoid blaming [22]. Some people tend to blame themselves for everything that goes wrong, not realizing that many circumstances are out of their control. For instance, you might blame yourself from someone's death and hate yourself, when you could not have prevented the death no matter what. You must realize that the world does not rest on your shoulders alone.

Others blame other people or life events for everything that goes wrong and don't accept control over their own lives. If you make a traffic mistake and get into a wreck, you blame the other driver for not braking in time. You harbor anger and resentment against everyone and you think that life isn't fair. You don't take control of your actions and apologize when you should. This fills your mind with hatred for the world around you.

You must strike a fine balance when it comes to assigning responsibility to yourself or others. Realize that you can and should take responsibility for your own actions. But sometimes things happen outside of your control. Really ask yourself if something was your fault or someone else's before casting unfair blame on the wrong party. In many cases, all parties were at fault, so there is no use blaming anyone. Instead of trying to find who is at fault or beating yourself up, think about solutions that can make the situation better.

Black and white thinking can drive negativity and bad self-talk, too [22]. This is a cognitive distortion where you feel that things are either all sunshine and rainbows, or all dark and evil. You ignore the gray area that exists in every part of life. For instance, if someone does something bad to you, you think he or she is an evil person. In reality, people are always a mixture of good and bad.

By accepting the fact that things are not black and white, you can stop dwelling on negative emotions like hatred and anger. Let go of the idea that something is all bad and try to find good in it to lessen your reaction to it. You can also stave off reckless optimism that leads to heartbreak and disappointment by accepting that nothing and no one is perfect. There will be something bad or less than ideal about everything and everyone in life. As long as you can focus on the good, you can achieve more positivity and happiness in your attitude.

In some cases, the bad always outweighs the good. If you are dating someone and you can't think of too many good things about him or her, that is a sign that the relationship is not right for you. Instead of blaming yourself or demonizing the other person, simply accept that it is time to move on. Find a healthier situation. Use gray area thinking to recognize when things no longer serve you and you need to move on in life. Don't let bad things fill you with rancor; simply accept that they are bad and that better is waiting for you somewhere else.

Objective Criticism

Pointing out the bad in yourself is not always a bad thing. In fact, it can be quite helpful in driving positive self-growth and change. Objective criticism is the ability to see problems in yourself and address them. It is different from negative self-talk because it is actually helpful. It leads you to find solutions to your behavior and flaws to lead a better life, as opposed to just beating yourself up like with negative self-talk.

An example of objective criticism is the thinking that led you to read this book. You realized that you have a problem with negative self-talk. You recognized that your thinking was causing disturbances in your life and preventing you from being fulfilled. So, you decided to do something about it.

Another example might be when you get into a fight with your spouse. Afterward, you feel awful and you want to say sorry. You see that you did something wrong and you sought to make it right.

Or let's say you are an author. You have sent your book out to a million publishers and received nothing but rejections. As a result, you decide to improve your book. You don't sit there feeling sorry for yourself and thinking that you should give up writing. Instead, you recognized that you have potential but you are missing the mark, so you do something to achieve your goal of publication.

Objective criticism starts with realizing that you are not perfect; no one is. You accept that about yourself and don't let it hurt you. You also forgive yourself and believe in your ability to improve. You know that you have the capability within yourself to become better.

The next part involves identifying a problem or flaw in yourself. Some healthy introspection should reveal a few things that you could fix about yourself. After all, no one is perfect. Even people with high self-esteem are capable of seeing issues within themselves. The crucial difference here between negative self-talk and objective criticism is that you are able to focus on finding a solution, instead of beating yourself up and calling yourself names.

From there, you generate a plan on how you will address this problem and make it better. You set the plan into motion to achieve better results in life. You actively work on it, encouraging yourself and believing in yourself every day.

You may use object criticism on yourself. Or you may receive it from someone else. When you hear someone say something negative about you, you don't get offended, Instead, you choose to use their suggestions as motivation to change. Basically, objective criticism is the same as constructive criticism, except you use it on yourself. You gently point out flaws and suggest improvements.

Objective criticism is useless if you don't use it as a foundation for betterment. Sitting there thinking about how you messed up does not do a single thing. But realizing that you goofed and then taking action to correct that goof is useful. Objective criticism is a powerful tool that can drive positive change within your life.

However, you may also use to accept yourself completely as you are. You may find a few things that you don't necessarily like about yourself. But they have served you thus far. You don't really want to change them. In that case, use object criticism to point out the silver lining to your flaws and embrace them as parts of you. Come to terms with the fact that you are not perfect.

Many people tend to be perfectionists. This only creates the ideal environment for negative self-talk to brew, like bacteria in lukewarm meat. As you set unrealistic high standards for yourself, you are always disappointed. This makes you start to hate yourself because you never live up to your expectations. With objective criticism, you can realize this about yourself and decide to set your standards lower. If you are never good enough, maybe it is time to stop expecting so much of yourself. Accept that you are only human.

However, it is healthy to think, "I am capable of doing the best." That serves as a source of motivation to always do better. By believing in yourself, you eliminate the negative thoughts that lie under perfectionism and instead generate positive thoughts that lie under success.

Objective criticism can also drive good work. Analyze the work you have performed. See where there is room for improvement. Use feedback from others and your own inner critic to make the work as good as it can possibly be. Don't just beat yourself up for not doing something exquisite the first try. Many people with high self-esteem excel in business because they are able to say, "This isn't quite good enough." But they don't just give up and think, "I can never do this." They keep working at it, believing that they can do better. Objective criticism is founded in a sense of confidence, not a sense of inadequacy.

No one enjoys hearing or thinking that he or she is not good enough. But if you speak to yourself nicely and focus on solutions rather than problems, you tend to handle it more gracefully and feel less pain. Just as you would use tact in pointing out something negative to a friend, use tact with yourself. There is no need to critique yourself sharply and harshly. Using gentle language, tell yourself how you can do better and formulate a plan.

You can even use a visualization to picture how you could become the ideal version of yourself or produce better work. Compare reality to your dream. See how they don't match up and then make them match up. Use your inner critic to fuel your motivation to thrive in life.

The Self-Talk Checklist

A checklist can make it easy to redirect your thoughts because you don't have to scramble to remember everything you must do in the construction of positive self-talk. Go down this checklist and see what you did in your positive self-talk. Try to incorporate the elements of the checklist in future positive self-talk.

✓ Is your self-talk stated in the present tense?

6. Talking about the future or the past won't do you any good. The only moment your brain can control is now. Therefore, your self-talk should be based in the present. Think things like, "I am good enough" as opposed to "I will be good enough."

7.

✓ Is it specific?

8. Your self-talk needs to be specific. Tell yourself exactly what you're good at or what you did well. You will believe it more if it is specific.

9.

✓ Does it get the job done without creating any unwanted side effects?

10.

11. Self-talk that unintentionally makes you feel bad is still negative self-talk. You might tell yourself something like "I tried my best" which makes you think that you didn't actually do your best, for example.

12.

✓ Is it easy to use?

13.   Self-talk that is not clear or simple will not work. Your brain will have too much trouble processing it, so it won't internalize the meaning behind it and actually believe it. Simple phrases and thoughts are ideal.

14.

✓ Is it practical?

15.   Wildly unrealistic self-talk will only set you up for failure. Focus on things that are tangible and real. For example, telling yourself that you are the best may not be believable, but telling yourself that you are good enough is.

16.

✓ Is it personal?

17.   Your self-talk needs to be about you and things that are profound to you. You need to focus on issues of deep personal significance to yourself. Telling yourself that you are good enough when that is not your real insecurity won't do any good. Find what does cause great insecurity within you and build your self-talk around increasing your confidence in that area.

18.

    ✓ Is it honest?

19.   Don't lie to yourself. Your self-talk needs to be honest. While it must be positive, it is OK to use objective criticism, as covered in the last section of this chapter.

20.

    ✓ Does your self-talk ask enough of you?

21.   Self-talk is not helpful if it doesn't push you to succeed. Challenge yourself and really believe that you can rise to the challenge.

22.

    ✓ Does your self-talk make you feel good?

23.   Your goal with positive self-talk is to encourage yourself to go far. You want to feel lifted up, encouraged, and excited after giving yourself a pep talk. Self-talk that doesn't make you feel good doesn't belong in your mind. Use thought stopping to cease it and find something more positive to center your thoughts around.

24.

    ✓ Does your self-talk encourage you to go for

better?

25. You can't love yourself if you don't push yourself to be the best version that you can be. Your self-talk can ask a lot of you, as long as it's realistic and not punishing. Higher expectations can push you to do better. Don't fall into the trap of expecting yourself to be perfect and then beating yourself up when you fall short of those unrealistic expectations, however.

26.

✓ Does your self-talk encourage you to leave or protect yourself from toxic situations?

27. Self-talk is not helpful if you are simply convincing yourself that a bad situation is good. Acknowledge your true feelings. If someone or something is hurting you, you must believe that you don't deserve it. Stop rationalizing it and acknowledge your pain and your desire for something better.

28.

✓ Do you actually believe it?

29. If your self-talk sounds hollow and you don't

believe it, ask yourself why. You may need to do some introspective exploring to get to the root of your problems.

30.

✓ Do you have evidence to support it?

31. Evidence can make self-talk more convincing and impactful. For instance, look at a trophy on the wall that you earned or your college diploma. Remember that you earned that. Seek evidence for why you are worthy or good enough or whatever else you are trying to work on.

32.

✓ Are you focused on finding a solution?

33. If you are talking yourself through a problem, your true goal should be to find a viable solution. Only then can you feel better about your life, because you fixed an issue for yourself. That grows your confidence. Solution-oriented thinking also really helps you take the emotion out of the equation and focus on logic instead, so you feel less hurt and anxious.

34.

✓ Are you trying to find a silver lining in a bad situation?

35. Positive self-talk is not the same as denial. If you are in an unpleasant situation, you must get out of it for your own health and safety. Don't let self-talk convince you to ignore red flags and unhappiness.

36.

✓ Are you casting blame on yourself or another person?

37. As you read before, there is no room for blame. It only causes hard feelings and often it is misplaced. Instead, focus on finding solutions. Don't point fingers at other people and hate them, and don't beat yourself up.

38.

✓ Are you letting go of unwanted feelings?

39. When you feel negative, that can breed negative self-talk. The best way to stop negative self-talk is to let go of the negative feelings and invite warm, happy feelings. Meditation or visualization or priming can help you achieve this.

40.

    ✓ Are you stopping negative thoughts and chasing them with positive ones?

41.   For every negative thought, there is an equally positive one. Identify the negatives ones and chase them with positive ones to make positive thinking a habit. You are reprogramming your brain this way. Identify some common negative thoughts you have and then think of more positive ones that you can use to follow these bad thoughts. Get into the habit of thinking these positives thoughts whenever the negative ones occur.

42.

    ✓ Are you believing what someone else has said about you?

43.   What people say about you is not true. They don't know you like you know you. While people can offer some valid clues about how you should change, mostly they are taking their own frustrations or insecurities out on you. Don't let negative words get to you and don't let manipulators charm you. Form your own idea of

who you are and don't let others influence it, positively or negatively. A sense of independence and separateness from others is essential to staying true to yourself.

44.

✓ Is your self-talk actionable?

45. Backing your self-talk up with action makes it more effective in changing your life. You will learn more about this, but make sure to have actionable plans when you talk to yourself. Tell yourself how you might address something, or plan a way to treat yourself and make yourself feel better.

46.

✓ Are you motivating yourself?

47. Before a big show, event, or presentation, it is key to motivate yourself with a little pep talk and some upbeat music. You can also try to use this when you feel anxious about a life event, such as taking a job offer or getting married. Ease anxiety by instead motivating yourself to take action and do something great. Always build yourself up with self-talk when you feel nervous to increase

confidence and success, the way Olympic athletes and professional dart players do.

48.

✓ Are you acknowledging your real feelings?

49.　Your real feelings are important clues as to how your life is going. They can alert you to danger, toxic situations, or situations that just aren't the right fit for you at this time. Don't ignore them or soothe them away. Acknowledge them and let yourself feel them. Then tell yourself it's OK to feel that way and find a way to feel better.

50.

✓ Are you speaking to yourself like a friend?

51.　Bad words, insults, and harsh reprimands are not how you should talk to yourself. Stop those thoughts immediately. You must be kind to yourself. Speak to yourself like an old friend that you truly cherish.

52. **Chapter 4: Take Action Now**

53. Positive thinking can bring about some great changes in your life. But it is not going to do a whole lot of good if you don't back positive self-talk and positive thinking with real actions. You can think all day, but only actions will actually trigger positive change in your life.

54.

55. Positive thinking and positive self-talk can lift the haze of depression that keeps you from taking action. It can also serve as a fantastic source of motivation. It is an excellent place to start in changing your life, which is why it is so crucial to practice.

56.

57. But now, you need to take it a step further by taking action. Otherwise, your life will not change. You can sit in your armchair and think happy thoughts but that won't make a bit of difference. If you get up and do something to make you happy, however, you will see results. Don't believe that good things come to those who wait. Good things

come to those who work for it. Work for a better life by doing some of the following things.

58.

Make Amends

One major source of the internal conflict that leads to negative self-talk is feeling guilty for some of your less-than-savory actions. All of us have made mistakes, so this does not mean that you are a terrible person. However, the way you handle your mistakes defines how you view yourself and how you feel about your past.

Eliminate regrets and the negative self-talk they generate by making amends for the wrongs you have committed. Say sorry to someone you hurt. Reach out to that old friend that you miss and say "I miss you."

Another thing to do is to ask people for apologies. This may sound crazy because most people who don't love themselves never think to do this. But you can heal a lot of old wounds by telling someone how they hurt you and asking for an apology. You might not hear that apology, but you just got your pent-up anger and hurt off of your chest. Plus, many people don't mean to hurt you and they will be more than happy to make amends to wrongs they didn't mean to commit. Some people may be scared to talk to you after they wronged you, so they appreciate the invitation to be forgiven.

Go After Your Dream Career

A huge act of self-love is finally making that career move that you have been too scared to make. Opening your own business, leaving a corporate job to make art or freelance, leaving your comfortable job of many years for a bigger one, asking your boss for a promotion – these are all scary things. People who don't' love themselves assume that they can't succeed, so they don't take the scary step. They live in fear forever.

However, if you love yourself, you know that you can do it. You also know that your happiness is not a luxury, but an imperative key to your life. Positive self-talk can help you love yourself enough to take that big step and give yourself something that you really want.

Think about how you want your career to change. Then list the steps you need to make to change it. Put those steps into a plan that you start to work on now. Through deliberate moves, you can make your dreams come true.

When an opportunity comes along, don't hang back in fear. Think, "I deserve this. This is the payout for how hard I've worked." Seize the opportunity and make the best of it.

Fear of the unknown is natural. As your own best friend, however, you will have the confidence to face the unknown. Making a big life change is an act of self-love and you will survive it. Remove the catastrophic sense from the equation and instead think about how great things could be if they worked out. Then take the risk and find out for yourself if this new opportunity is for you or not.

Get Physically Active

Exercise is a simple yet huge act of self-care. There are countless benefits to exercise. For one thing, exercise reduces the stress hormone cortisol, which can make you sleep better and feel better in general [23]. Exercise also stabilizes other hormones, so your mood can improve [23]. On top of weight loss benefits, exercise can increase insulin sensitivity, which can help you absorb nutrients from your food and get nourishment better while banishing tiredness [23]. It can reduce the risk of diseases like Type 2 diabetes and heart disease and even cancer [23]. As your body gets toned, you will have a better self-image and more confidence. You may even make friends at your new workout class or gym.

Most experts recommend at least 150 minutes of

exercise per week [23]. How you get this exercise depends on what you like. You will stick to exercise that you enjoy more than something you hate. Any kind of movement will be beneficial in the long run.

Eat Better

Like exercise, eating a good diet is essential to your health and your self-care. You can gain health and lose weight by eating better. Cut out junk food and limit portions. Choose healthy whole foods that you actually like. There is no need to starve yourself or eat health food that you detest, but take care to keep your diet clean. Your sense of well-being and happiness will flourish as you nourish your body the right way. Different people need different diets, so speak to a nutritionist to find the ideal eating plan for your body type and lifestyle.

Start A Fun Hobby

Hobbies are also great for your mental well-being and

can relax you after a long day of work or parenting. Doing something that you enjoy is important for your overall health. Find something that you have been wanting to try and try it. If you don't like it, you can stop. Try different hobbies until you find one that you care about.

You should also take an old hobby that you neglected out of busyness. If you miss doing something, make the time to do it. Tell yourself, "I owe this to myself. I can find some time on the weekend to fish again."

Connect With New People

Part of the self-love that comes with positive self-talk involves being more confident and more popular as a result. Your newfound positivity draws people to you. This can make your social life infinitely better.

Take the time to connect with new people. Chat with people you already know but don't connect with much. Call up an old friend. Go out and meet new people with new events or hobbies. As you make more friends, you will feel more likable, which can make you like yourself more. New friends can also open up opportunities for you.

Read A Book Or Watch A Movie You've Been Putting Off

To relax, you should take in a book or movie that you have been wanting to enjoy. Allowing yourself time to enjoy art of some kind is key to unwinding and adding beauty to your life. Just a few minutes to a few hours will renew your appreciation for the world.

In fact, looking at art can have some positive implications for the brain [24]. Art tends to stimulate the release of dopamine in the brain, which makes you feel happier [24]. Art therapy has been used for decades to treat depression, PTSD, anxiety disorder, eating disorders, and other mental health issues for good reason.

Art can range from appreciating a good piece of cinematography to looking at pictures in a gallery. It can involve cozying up with a good book or creating jewelry. Whatever you like that involves art, do it to get a healthy dose of dopamine in your brain.

Travel

Not everyone loves traveling. So if traveling is not for you, there is no need to do it. However, most people have some wanderlust in their hearts. They don't travel out of fear, or because they are too busy, or because they don't have enough money.

Nevertheless, if you start to stop fear and instead build courage with positive self-talk, you can make anything possible. You can find a way to set aside time and raise money for that dream trip. Traveling is a great reward to yourself, to pay yourself back for your hard work and let yourself see the world. It will expose you to new situations and allow you to test yourself, proving a lot to yourself in the process.

Unabashedly Seek Help

If the work required in developing positive self-talk unearths some serious issues, such as mental illness or trauma that you have not healed from, then don't feel ashamed about seeking help.

While a stigma surrounds mental health, there is truly nothing wrong with it. It is better to be healthy and treat mental health issues than to act out on them or let them ruin your life and your relationships. Untreated mental illness can lead to substance abuse, self-harm, suicide, and bad relationships, so you can hurt yourself and others. You can do everyone a favor, including yourself, by committing to a treatment program.

A professional counselor or therapist can help you achieve self-love by offering an outside perspective. A psychiatrist can prescribe medication to aid you in recovering from mental illness and gaining the chemical balance essential to positive thinking.

Use Assertive Language

There are several conversation styles that people adopt [25]. Sometimes, one's style may change, depending on the audience. But the single most effective communication style is assertiveness.

With assertiveness, you are not passive. You tell people what you need or what you feel without fear. However, you do it in a tactful way, not an aggressive way. Hence, you manage to assert boundaries, get what you need, make people respect you, and avoid making enemies or hurting people.

An act of self-care is adopting assertive language. You

want to speak firmly. State what you need. Don't hem and haw, but be clear. If something is bothering you, don't hold it in, or act emotionally. Just say what is on your mind and suggest a way to make it better.

It is possible to stage conflict without anyone getting hurt. You can tell people how you feel and ask them to treat you better without yelling, screaming, manipulating, or crying. Such is the beauty of assertive language. You want to be clear about what you are saying. You also want to listen to what your conversation partner says and repeat it back to him to ensure that you get the message.

To speak assertively, make direct eye contact at all times. Speak calmly, without raising your voice, but enunciate clearly. Say what you mean in as few as words as possible; don't make flowery speeches.

Say you feel passed over at work. You can be assertive by asking to speak to your boss. Look him in the eye and say, "I appreciate all that you have done for me and I love working here. But I feel passed over for this project. I feel that I have many things to offer this project, and I should be chosen." Then give your boss time to reply.

Or say your partner carelessly makes a comment about your clothes that hurts your feelings. You can look him or her in the eye and say, "That was hurtful and I don't appreciate it." You don't need to yell, sulk, or cry. Just make your feelings apparent. Give your partner time to apologize and fix what he or she said.

If someone keeps bothering you, you can say, "I really don't like when you do that. Could you please stop?" There is nothing aggressive with that message. It simply gets the message across in an assertive way.

Never level accusations, such as "You keep doing that!" This puts a person on the defensive. Instead, say, "I don't like when you do that." "I messages" are important in assertive language because it makes what you're saying about you, not about the other person. That removes defensiveness and the need for conflict.

People generally respond well to assertiveness. They like to be given clear directions. Most people will obey what you say if you say it politely but assertively.

Set Boundaries With People

A huge source of unhappiness for most people is a lack of boundaries. Using the assertive language that you learned about earlier, you can draw clear boundaries to keep people from infringing on your values or your personal space. That way, you become happier.

Often, people don't do this because they are afraid of making others not like them. Now that you are your own best friend, you don't need other people to like you to feel validated as a good person. In fact, as you set boundaries in relationships, many people will start to like you more because they can respect you and they know how to act around you.

Your boundaries may be very different from someone else's. It is important to be honest with yourself and get to know the rules you want to set. What bothers you? What is OK and what is not? When people violate these boundaries, firmly but politely speak up and ask the person not to do it again.

End Some Toxic Relationships

It is time to make a list of the people in your life who hurt you. Figure out why each person hurts you. Maybe the problem is you; you take what this person says too personally or you don't communicate well, or you harbor some jealousy because you are engaged in evaluating yourself against this person. But some people are just downright toxic and hurtful, and it is not your fault.

It is crucial to cut these people out of your life. The people who tear you down or make you feel bad when you spend time with them are not good for your health. You don't owe them anything. Do yourself a favor and remove contact with them.

Sometimes, it is not possible to just cut a toxic person from your life. Perhaps you have a co-worker, an in-law, or some other such person that is in your daily life and you cannot create distance. In this case, simply minimize contact and avoid him or her for the most part. When this person hurts you, use visualization to neutralize your feelings and make them less severe and personal. Use a mantra or affirmation to reassure yourself after dealing with this person.

Practice Saying No

Too many people neglect the word "no" in their vocabulary. You want to please other people to gain validation for yourself. Consequently, you overextend yourself, letting people walk all over you and taking on more tasks than you fit on your plate at the moment. You end up exhausted and regretful at the sharp lack of time you leave for yourself. You feel that no one is truly grateful for all that you do.

Assure yourself that you don't need to make other people like you by doing them favors. Favors only invite people to use you. Instead, you can make people like you by being yourself and letting your good qualities shine through.

Practice looking at your schedule and determining if you really have time to help someone or take on more at work. If a new favor or project cuts into your self-care time, such as your yoga class, put yourself first and say no. Go to yoga. Don't commit to someone else's problems.

You should also say no to things or people that hurt you. If you have a toxic family member who asks to stay, you might feel obligated to say yes, even though you know the stay won't be pleasant. Now, try saying no. Conserve your time and space for yourself and avoid the people who bring you down. If you feel obligated to go to a party but you don't really want to go, then say no. You don't have to please others by showing up to events that you hate.

Practice Saying Yes

While no is a very important word in anyone's vocabulary, so is yes. Too many say no when they want to say yes. They let fear and uncertainty prevent them from agreeing to a situation, person, or opportunity that could potentially change their lives for the better.

Using self-talk, you can gain more confidence and ease social anxiety. This, in turn, can help you find the courage to say yes to that masquerade ball, that new hobby, or that hot date. If you feel a spark in your heart that urges you to say yes, then say yes! Don't let the negative self-doubt make you say no instead.

Conclusion

You are sick of calling yourself names and believing the worst about yourself. Something told you to pick up this book, and now you have all of the tools necessary to reprogram your brain and end the nasty self-talk.

You now know how terrible self-talk is for you. Therefore, you understand it is imperative to switch to positive self-talk. Positive self-talk can make you happier and can enhance your performance in all areas of life. Using it will certainly elevate you to a better lifestyle.

However, just understanding the benefits of positive self-talk won't make it a viable habit. You must use repetition to make it a part of your daily life and enjoy its many benefits. Repeat it every day for 66 days to cement it as a new habit.

Right now, negative self-talk is your habit. It may have come from an abusive or invalidating childhood, or a traumatic event, or a loss. Whatever the cause, you are not benefiting from it anymore. You can erase the habit of negative thinking and start to enjoy life. Your physical and mental health will improve as a result.

You can reprogram your brain at any age because of neuroplasticity. With mantras, thought stopping, positive affirmations, mental decluttering, and avoiding cognitive distortions, you can reprogram your brain to be more positive. Soon, your instinct won't be to lash out at yourself. You will instead welcome very positive, solution-based approaches to life situations and calm acceptance of painful memories.

You can do most of this work on your own, without paying for an expensive therapist. CBT, visualization, and mental reprogramming are all techniques you can use on your own. However, don't be afraid to reach out for help if you need it. This book is not intended as a replacement for mental health or physical health treatment. To achieve the best results, stick with your current doctors' prescribed interventions and compound them with positive self-talk. You can even find a therapist or counselor who will help you achieve the mental reprogramming necessary for positive self-talk to become a part of your life.

Positive thinking is useless without action behind it. As you begin to talk to yourself as you would a best friend, you will find the motivation to treat yourself with love. This will spill over into your life. You will want to remove toxic situations and friendships from your life, forgive yourself and others, take advantage of great opportunities, and engage in healthy habits that make you happy. You will be able to heal old wounds and make amends. Through a series of actions, you can let positive self-talk make an actual difference in your life.

Be mindful that positivity does not equal happy all of the time. You can criticize yourself and feel pain still. You just have a healthier way to handle it now.

With positive self-talk, you can open many doors that have been closed for all of your life. Say hello to a bright and wonderful future. It starts today by implementing the techniques covered in these pages!

Resources

[1] Markham, Laura. Peaceful Parent, Happy Kids: How to Stop Yelling and Start Connecting. 2012. TarcherPerigee. ISBN-13: 978-0399160288.

[2] Burnett, Paul. Children's Self-Talk and Significant Others' Positive and Negative Statements. Educational Psychology. 1996. Vol 6, Issue 1. https://doi.org/10.1080/0144341960160105

[3] Kross, Ethan, et al. Self-Talk as a Regulatory Mechanism: How You Do It Matters. Journal of Personality and Social Psychology. American Psychological Association. 2014. Vol. 106, No. 2, 304–324. DOI:10.1037/a0035173

[4]. Yaratan, Huseyin. Self-esteem, self-concept, self-talk and significant others' statements in fifth grade students: Differences according to gender and school type. Procedia - Social and Behavioral

Sciences. 2010. Volume 2, Issue 2, pp. 3506-3518 https://doi.org/10.1016/j.sbspro.2010.03.543

[5] Making a Bad Situation Worse: How Negative Self-Talk Worsens Child Anxiety. *Child Anxiety Institute.* http://childrenwithanxiety.com/making-a-bad-situation-worse-how-negative-self-talk-worsens-child-anxiety.html.

[6] Young, Jeffrey & Klosko, Janet. *Reinventing Your Life.* 1994. ASIN: B0776JJ6L8.

[7] Goodhart, D. *Some psychological effects associated with positive and negative thinking about stressful event outcomes: was Pollyanna right?*

Journal of Personal Social Psychology. Vol 48, Issue 1, pp. 216-232. DOI: https://www.ncbi.nlm.nih.gov/pubmed/398

1389.

[8] Allan, Scott. *Rejection Reset*. 2017. ASIN: B075JMRTL2.

[9] Zinsser, N., Bunker, L.K, & Williams, J.M. Cognitive techniques for improving performance and building confidence. In J.M. Williams (Ed.), Applied Sport Psychology: Personal growth to peak performance (5th Ed.). McGraw-Hill College, 2006.

[10] Mann, Michael, et al. Self-Esteem in a Broad-Spectrum Approach for Mental Health Promotion. Health Education Research. 2004. Vol 19, No 4, pp. 357-372.

[11] Collingwood, Jane. The Relationships Between Mental and Physical Health. 2018. PsychCentral. https://psychcentral.com/lib/the-relationship-between-mental-and-physical-

health/

[12] Raalte, JV. Et al. Cork! The Effects of Positive and Negative Self-Talk on Dart Throwing Performance. Journal of Sport Behavior. 1995. Vol 18, Issue 1.

[13] Chapman University. New Research on Attractiveness and Mating. ScienceDaily. https://www.sciencedaily.com/releases/201 5/09/150916162912.htm.

[14] Gardner, Benjamin, et al. Making Health Habitual. British Journal of General Practice. 2012. Vol 62, No 605, pp. 664-666.

[15] Jones, MD, et al. A naturalistic study of fat talk and its behavioral and affective consequences. Body Image. 2014. Vol 11, No 4, pp. 337-345. doi: 10.1016/j.bodyim.2014.05.007.

[16] Miller, Kevin, et al. Habits without Values. Cold Spring Harbor Laboratory. 2018. doi: https://doi.org/10.1101/067603.

[17] Demartini, John. The Demartini Method. https://drdemartini.com/about/demartini-method/

[18] Robbins, Tony. How Should I Start Each Day? What's Priming? https://www.tonyrobbins.com/ask-tony/priming/

[19] Bandler, Richard. The Ultimate Guide to NLP: How to Build a Successful Life. 2013. HarperCollins. ISBN-13: 978-0007497416

[20] Schacter, Daniel L., et al. The Future of Memory: Remembering, Imagining, and the Brain. 2013. Neuron. Vol 76, No 4. doi: 10.1016/j.neuron.2012.11.001

[21] Stop Negative Thoughts. *Michigan Medicine.* 2019. https://www.uofmhealth.org/health-library/uf9938.

[22] Wolf, Alex. *Cognitive Behavioral Therapy: An Effective Practical Guide for Rewiring Your Brain and Regaining Control over Anxiety, Phobias, and Depression.* ISBN13: 9781726691222.

[23] *Benefits of Exercise.* MedlinePlus. https://medlineplus.gov/benefitsofexercise.html

[24] Regev, Dafna, et al. *Effectiveness of Art Therapy in Adults in 2018 – What Progress Has Been Made?* Frontier Psychology. 2018. Vol 9, p. 1531. DOI: 10.3389/fpsyg.2018.01531

[25] Newton, Claire. *The Five Conversation Skills.* Web. N.d.

http://www.clairenewton.co.za/my-articles/the-five-communication-styles.html.

The Power Of Self-Talk

How To Stop Beating Yourself Up, Take Action And Achieve Success In Your Life

By

Stuart Wallace

Introduction

The endless loop of negative thinking plagues you from day to day. You feel that you can't do anything right and you believe that you are a horrible person. Sometimes, you wonder if there was a way to break through the negative self-talk and make yourself more successful.

You can stop wondering. There is indeed a great way to bring about success in all areas of your life. The way is positive self-talk.

I was raised in a negative environment. Hence, my mind was programmed to think negatively. I would beat myself up every chance I got, and I would hang back from success at work and in my love life by telling myself that I wasn't able to achieve my dreams. When I discovered positive self-talk in a CBT course, I thought, "Is there something significant here?" Building off of the course, I began to learn more about positive self-talk. Now I am married to the woman of my dreams, I have completed my graduate degree, and I have earned several promotions at work. All of my success centers around my new way of talking to myself.

Your life is built around the kind of thoughts you think. You inadvertently sabotage everything you want for yourself with negative thinking and self-doubt. By using positive self-talk, you can change your life around. From improving relationships with your family to earning a promotion at work to opening your own business, you can motivate yourself with positive self-talk. Success is not for the privileged few; it is for everyone who works for it. With a little concentrated work on your self-talk, you can make all of your dreams come true and break out of the cycle of negative self-talk that is holding you back.

This book is the solution to the negative self-talk that keeps you stuck in the same miserable state, day after day, year after year. You obviously want your life to change for the better, or you wouldn't be reading this book. Success can be yours when you apply the concepts in this book to your family, your love life, your social life, and your business or work.

I promise you that by the time you finish this book, you will know how to change your life around. You will be able to achieve everything you keep telling yourself is not possible. Motivation and success will be yours for the taking.

If you keep engaging in negative self-talk, you will continue to be unhappy. You will continue to be passed over for promotions or raises at work, you will continue to put your goals on hold, and you will continue to receive social and romantic rejections. Problems within your family, such as fighting, will also continue. But if you take action now, you can solve all of these problems and more.

Don't hesitate. Start working on your self-talk today and you will see enormous benefits. Read on to grow your self-esteem, become motivated, and reach new levels of success that you never imagined were possible. You can change your present state of negativity, but only if you start working on it now!

Chapter 1: What Is Positive Self-Talk?

What is this positive self-talk I keep speaking about? As you have probably noticed, you tend to talk to yourself. It's not crazy – everyone does it. A constant narrative runs in your mind, telling you what to do, informing you of who you are. The voice may sound like your own, or like someone else's, such as a parent or teacher you once had. The voice may change tone and message depending on your mood and situation.

This is your self-talk. It is your brain's way of directing your actions and processing the information you receive from the world around you in a way it can handle [1]. Your self-talk may be negative, in that you tell yourself bad things, call yourself names, or dwell on bad things that have happened to you. Or it could be positive, always uplifting you with encouraging words. Positive self-talk is obviously the better of the two forms of self-talk, as it motivates you to do your best and keeps your mood bright.

Now chances are, if you are reading this, you already have a profound familiarity with negative self-talk. It has probably plagued you for years. You tell yourself that you can't do things. You insult and berate yourself for every mistake. Constantly, you are in a bad mood because your mind tells you awful things. You know that this self-talk is toxic, yet you can't seem to change it.

The truth is that you *can* change your self-talk. Through some work, you can reprogram your mind to think more positively. I know this is possible because I did it myself. I won't lie and claim that changing your thinking is the easiest thing in the world, but I do know that you can make it happen through repetition and other techniques that I cover throughout this book. In addition, I know that the benefits are tremendous in all areas of life. Changing your self-talk from negative to positive is certainly worth the effort.

To start the process of motivating yourself and gaining success through positive self-talk, you need to make a goal now: "I will start talking to myself like I am my own best friend."

That is the essence of positive self-talk. You build yourself up, instead of tearing yourself down. You think thoughts centered around how great of a person you are and how you can handle any challenge that life throws at you. You treat yourself like a best friend, encouraging and pushing yourself through life's hardest moments and biggest struggles. When you feel bad, you lift yourself up and seek comfort in healthy activities.

Positive self-talk is not thinking happy thoughts all of the time. It is more than possible to criticize yourself and correct your mistakes or reflect on how bad a problem is at the present moment. However, you do these things in a way that makes you feel better. You focus on solutions, rather than problems, and you don't hurt your self-esteem by repeating hurtful observations or insults to yourself.

When And Where Is Self-Talk Helpful?

We all have areas of life that can benefit and flourish from positive self-talk. As you learn to use positive self-talk, you will notice that all areas of your life improve. This is because your self-talk influences your attitude, and your attitude influences your actions. Having a positive attitude will cause you to act in ways that bring greater rewards to you than a negative attitude.

The first and foremost place where positive self-talk brings about good change is within yourself. Your self-esteem and confidence will grow. You will suddenly have the self-love required to take big risks and mitigate the problems that may arise in life. Fear will melt away, replaced by a self-assurance that you can do anything you set your mind to. You will instantly start to feel better about who you are as a person, how you look, what you have done in the past, and how you will tackle your dreams.

This has a trickledown effect in every other aspect of your life. Your interpersonal relationships, such as your friendships and familial relationships, will suddenly improve. This is because you show the ones you love more positivity and you become pleasanter to be around. You also handle interpersonal conflicts more effectively because you are no longer plagued by insecurities. Issues like jealousy or taking things too personally will fade away because you have more self-esteem. Your positive attitude will make you a more patient parent, and you will teach your kids better life skills by modeling positive self-talk for them.

You will also have the confidence to build new relationships. You will no longer want to hang back in shyness because you believe that you are a likable person. Other people will enjoy getting to know you. Your social circle will grow.

You will enjoy a better love life and more dates if you are still single. You will finally have the self-esteem that others find more attractive, plus you will smile more. If you are already married, you will have more fun with your spouse and bring more friendships into your life. This will make you a better spouse. I was single and suffering from constant romantic rejections when I was stuck in the negative self-talk loop; I was often stood up! Then I began to believe in my worthiness and I was able to attract my wife. Now she and I have many friends and enjoy many activities outside of our home, separate and together. Having these activities and friends makes our marriage fun and exciting.

With improved social relations, you will open up more opportunities and fewer conflicts. You can find people who will help you succeed in life and make them want to work with you. Potential clients will find you more likable, and therefore you will make more money. My improved social skills and positive attitude have made it possible for me to form many lucrative work relationships.

This can drastically improve your work life and your performance. You will also have more confidence to attract new clients, tackle bigger projects, and take more calculated risks. Your boss will notice your heightened work ethic, and you can expect promotions or raises. Climbing up the corporate ladder starts with believing that you are destined for the top.

If you want to start your own business or go after a new job, you will have the confidence to do so. You know that you can achieve what you want in life. But you also know that if you are rejected by a potential job or if your business fails, you won't be failing at life. You can get back up from rejection and failure with less pain and you can learn from your mistakes in order to do better in the future. This self-assurance and self-love make you able to take on risks that can move your life forward. You are not really going after your dreams if you don't take some risks.

For instance, I took a big risk when I decided to leave a job I hated and start a freelance career. I didn't know if I would even be able to pay the bills with a freelance job, but I thought I might as well try. Before I started positive self-talk, I wanted to try freelancing but I kept telling myself that I would probably fail at it and end up bankrupt. After starting positive self-talk, I was able to convince myself that I had every skill necessary to make freelancing work. Then I started and I enjoyed far more success than I thought possible.

Eventually, I decided to make freelancing a side gig and went after a job with a Fortune 500 company. Again, I didn't think I could get it, but I assured myself that it would not hurt to try. My palms sweat and I trembled in my shoes in the lobby as I wanted to be taken in for my interview. Was my resume good enough? Was my freelance experience something that could be taken seriously? I kept reminding myself that I had what it took for the job and I was the best candidate out of all my competition. I was dressed for success and I had a smile plastered on my face. *I got this,* I kept telling myself.

Guess what? I got the job and I have received two promotions in two years. Was I fearless? Absolutely not. But I used positive self-talk to make something great out of that fear.

Chapter 2: You Are What You Think

Je pense, donc je suis. "I think, therefore I am." This phrase is famous because it is true. Our ability to reason and apply logic or emotion to situations makes us human.

But the reverse is also true: You are what you think. The thoughts that go through your mind define you and instruct your brain to view you in a certain light. Hence, changing your thoughts can change who you are.

You would not be who you are today if not for your self-talk. Now you must ask yourself: Am I happy the way I am? If you are depressed, fatigued, and lacking in confidence because of negative self-talk, you are not being your best self. You have so much potential that you bury underneath thoughts like, "I couldn't possibly do that" or "I don't have what it takes." You turn down great opportunities out of fear, you ignore great people because you don't think you're worthy of their friendship, and you drive people who love you away with your negativity and insecurities. That is not how you become successful and win at life.

When you change your internal dialogue from negative to positive, you also change the way you feel and act. You feel better, and thus you project positivity outward. This makes the world kinder to you.

I bet you know someone who always seems positive and upbeat. This person brightens the room when he or she walks in. This person also seems to get what he or she wants without too much effort. Things always work out for this person – even bad things tend to turn out positive in the end for him or her.

Instead of feeling jealous of this person, think about how you can be more like him or her. This enviable person simply has a positive mindset that unlocks doors for him or her in all areas of life. This person doesn't let negative thinking ruin everything. He or she also doesn't engage in comparisons and feel inadequate next to others. "I can do it" seems to be this person's mantra in life. By adopting a similar mindset and self-talk, you can certainly make yourself like this person, always attracting good things in life and radiating positivity.

Now let's consider the science behind why the energy of your self-talk makes such a huge difference in your quality of life.

How Does Self-Talk Work?

Your self-talk serves as a regulatory mechanism, which your brain employs to make decisions [1]. Self-talk is an introspective tool, which influences your attitude, behavior, and beliefs [1]. Your brain basically tells itself something to reinforce a belief and instruct your subsequent actions.

Self-talk reinforces your brain's idea of who you are, and thus how you should act [1]. Self-talk makes it easy to determine how you should respond to a situation, because it upholds a sense of how you would normally act that fits neatly into your self-identity. Unfortunately, this can become problematic if your brain is regulating a self-identity that is negative.

The structure of your self-talk is built from your background and becomes a habit because this offers convenience for the brain [2]. If you don't have to think hard about what to say to yourself, your brain can save some serious effort. As your brain thinks a certain thought, it creates a neural pathway [2]. It is likely to follow this same neural pathway every time it encounters a situation that calls for a similar thought or decision. For instance, if you think "I'm an idiot!" when you make a big mistake at work, you tend to think that you're an idiot every single time you make a mistake because that is the easiest neural pathway available to the brain. Forcing yourself to think something more along the lines of, "That was a mistake but I can do better" can create a new (and more positive) neural pathway for your brain to take next time you screw up at work.

Habit change works on two of your brain's built-in decision-making systems, System 1 and System 2 [2]. System 1 is where you rely on old habits to make fast, almost automated decisions. You may beat yourself up for what you do using System 1 but beating yourself does not change System 1's wiring. System 2 is more conscious and deliberate and requires your brain to think hard. When you use System 2, you can make better decisions, which become habitual with repetition [2].

Think about what happens if you are going to a new address for the first time. Your brain saves the route as a neural pathway. This makes it easier for the brain to recall the route in the future. You keep taking that same route every time because your brain knows it. It is easier than forging new neural pathways by taking new routes. But if you keep taking new routes, then your brain gets used to it. With repetition, the pathways for different routes become "saved" in the brain and you can recall all of them when you have to decide which route to take during rush hour to save time.

Your memory works this same way and shapes your self-talk [3]. When you think on a memory, you are actually remembering the last time you thought about it. The same attitudes and feelings you experienced the last time you reflected on this memory will be instantly recalled. This can make you become stuck in a negative loop because you keep revisiting the same negative feelings every time you think back on a memory. You can continue to feel shame and humiliation about that time you puked on someone in high school for the rest of your life, which in turn lowers your self-esteem and mood and reinforces negative self-talk.

The cool thing about memory is that is not static, but rather adaptable [3]. Thinking about the memory in a new way can create a new neural pathway that triggers different feelings. Then, in the future, you have a better response to the memory. For example, when you recall that time your dog died, you naturally reflect on feeling terrible. You may blame yourself. In the future, you can reflect on how you did your best as a dog owner and gave your dog a good life. This makes the memory more bearable every time you think of it in the future, and thus you stop ruminating on how you failed.

Another interesting fact about memory is that your memories are not reliable. They are comprised of splinters of real events, distorted by your brain to fit your idea of reality [3]. Hence, your memories may be reworked to reinforce a negative idea you hold about yourself. Always remember that your memories are not accurate and things are probably not as bad as you are remembering them to be. You can reconstruct a memory as you see fit.

The brain works on a negative feedback loop system [4]. Basically, you have a picture of reality in your brain, which you started constructing as a baby. When your brain encounters situations that differ from this reality, it feels jarred and creates an irresistible urge to act in some way to "correct" the situation to fit into its neat little prepackaged picture. Maybe as a child your parent always told you that you were shy, so now that is your sense of your personal reality. When you are thrust into social situations, your brain thinks, "This isn't right. I'm shy. I'm not supposed to be outgoing in this situation." Thus, it tells you to act shyly in order to fit into its concept of reality. You can perpetuate negative behaviors as a result of this negative feedback system.

Your brain also relies on this negative feedback system to perpetuate your self-talk. When you encounter a situation, the brain tells itself to resort to its usual self-talk to regulate your behavior to match what your brain thinks is consistent for you [4]. Interestingly, serotonin can inhibit this [4]. Since serotonin is a neurochemical generated when you experience something positive, it follows that positive thinking can effectively rewire your brain. So, if you think things that make you happy, your brain starts to inhibit its own negative feedback loop system and rely on a new one that creates even more serotonin.

Changing your self-talk involves forging new neural pathways. This is why it can be difficult, at least at first, to make new self-talk habits. With time, however, your brain will get used to its new neural pathways built on positive thinking and it will start to follow them instead of the old negative routes. It will produce more serotonin which makes you happier as well.

You may have learned negative self-talk in the past. You probably learned it from a parent, who modeled negative self-talk for you, or you learned it from hearing someone criticize you a lot [1]. This formed a neural pathway of negative thinking that your brain takes every single time you have to think about yourself, following its System 1 decision-making loop [2]. It is a habit now. Your memories can also perpetuate negative self-talk as you recall unpleasant feelings and ideas about yourself based on the past [3]. But you can rework that habit and make your brain take a different route when you think about yourself in the future.

One of the best ways to change your thinking is to create self-distance [1]. You can also reprogram your brain by chasing negative thoughts with positive ones. Additionally, you can identify and undermine cognitive distortions that cause you to make poor decisions based on a distorted sense of reality [5]. Doing these two things can create new neural pathways that your brain will follow in the future. This can make positivity habit, thus removing your fallback of negative self-talk. Replacing bad feelings associated with memories can also help you feel better and create a more positive sense of identity that is less painful [3].

You will learn about how to do these things in more detail in Chapter 8, as well as throughout the following chapters.

Chapter 3: Consciously Rule Your Subconscious

Your subconscious is a deeply buried part of your brain, from which System 1 decisions are rapidly generated [2]. Your subconscious drives the thoughts you are consciously aware of. Thus, your self-talk is rooted in your subconscious. To reprogram it, you absolutely must use your conscious to drive home repeated new thoughts to reset the neural pathways that work behind the scenes in your subconscious mind.

Over the years, repeated exposure to negative inputs has created a negative System 1 program [2]. It only makes sense that you are now deeply engrained in negative self-talk. However, you can reprogram your brain with some work. You have to do reprogramming gradually; it does not work overnight. If you have gone through years of negative programming, positive reprogramming can take a while to become habitual. However, this habit is very beneficial because positive self-talk becomes the default for your brain. You will not have to think about it anymore once you reprogram your subconscious to rely on a positive thinking neural pathway.

What Positive Self-Talk Does For Your Brain

You have already learned about what positive self-talk does for your life. But we can go a little deeper by understanding how it affects your brain. Essentially, without going into a lengthy and boring text about neurochemistry, positive self-talk influences your brain's chemistry to make you feel better [6].

Positive self-talk has been linked to an improvement in depression and self-esteem [6]. It all boils down to how you choose to think about stressful events. Now it is true that your self-talk is driven behind the scenes by your negative feedback loop and your System 1 decision-making habits, but you can still make a conscious choice to change those thoughts.

That choice is reflected in your overall mood.

Positive self-talk helps you mitigate the toxic effects of stress from stressful events or situations [6]. As you think through bad things that have happened or are happening to you, you can ease the stress through positive self-talk. This has a wonderful effect on improving your mood and your overall mental health.

It also influences your physical health [6]. Depression and stress can lead to overeating or undereating, muscle aches, insomnia, and oversleeping. If you counter stress with soothing thinking and uplifting self-talk, you can see these symptoms start to vanish.

Positive self-talk also influences your performance. Olympic athletes often use it before a competition to win gold medals [7]. In fact, athletes have trained their brains so well that they can use a simple word to cue a flood of confidence before an event [7]. Dart players noticed higher scores when they practiced positive self-talk before league games [8]. By verbally building yourself up before an event or performance, you can really improve your odds of succeeding.

Furthermore, if you feel happy because you are thinking happier thoughts, you smile more. This makes you instantly more attractive to others [9]. In turn, you have more positive social experiences, which further elevates your self-esteem. It becomes a positive cycle that builds you up more and more.

Beating Negative Self-Talk Out Of Your Head

To effectively reprogram your subconscious, you must consciously think new thoughts. You can achieve reprogramming in a variety of ways, but the true secret is simple: Chase negative self-talk with positive self-talk and use a variety of tricks to induce positive self-talk so that it becomes habit. This can take some time and work, but if you set aside a block of time each day for 66 days to work on your self-talk, it will become a habit [2]. Using positive self-talk is a lifelong activity but it doesn't need to be strenuous, especially as it becomes habitual and automated.

Making a concentrated effort to think positively each day, especially when you encounter stress or negative circumstances, is something you must actively do for the rest of your life. Don't let this overwhelm you. Take it day by day and it will become a part of your normal thinking.

Create Self-Distance

The most constructive part of my self-talk journey was the day when I thought, "What is best for Jeffrey?" I referred to myself in the third person and stepped out of my mind for a moment to ponder what would be ideal for myself. Using an outside perspective, I was able to see what was obvious: I needed to go back to college. I had dropped out for a while and faced a series of setbacks in my career as a result. To further myself, I needed to complete my degree.

Inside my own mind, trapped behind the lens I always used to view my life, I knew completing my degree was necessary, but I kept clouding the idea out with negative self-talk, like "How can you possibly finish now? It costs too much, you don't have the time, and you dropped out before, so why would you finish now?" But when I stepped out of my own mind, I was able to see reality for what it was and make the best decision for myself. I was also able to determine how to reduce the cost of college and fit into my budget, how to make time for classes and studying, and how to motivate myself to stick with it to the end.

Positive self-talk is possible when you step out of the framework that you have erected around your identity. This process is called self-distance [1]. It involves looking at yourself as if through someone else's eyes. This removes the emotional and logical hurdles that you create for yourself based on your limited negative feedback loop system. It also helps you come up with new ideas and creative approaches that can help you overcome hurdles.

To create self-distance, first phrase your self-talk in the third person and call yourself by name [1]. This may feel weird, but that's just because your brain is not used to thinking like this. Ask yourself a series of questions targeted at discovering what is best for yourself:

- What is best for [your name]?
- What would make [your name] happy?
- What would solve his/her problem right now?
- What are the steps to accomplish this?
- What can [your name] do about this today?

When self-doubt or "What if" scenarios rear their heads, think about what someone else might say to those thoughts. For instance, when I thought "I can't afford college," I considered this from a college advisor's position and listed different ways I could. Financial aid, scholarships, and a careful budget immediately came to mind. I then thought "What if I take a loan out and can't get a job and pay the money back?" I reminded myself that people with college degrees make fifty percent more than those who don't to placate this fear.

Visualize

Many Olympic athletes use visualizations to make their goals seem more real to themselves [6]. When you visualize a goal, you can make it seem real to your brain. Then your brain believes that it can achieve success and you feel motivated.

Visualize what you want clearly. Envision how you will feel when you get what you want. Let that visualization motivate you. Whenever you feel discouraged or demoralized, fall back to that visualization to drive you forward.

Set Smart Goals

Part of positive self-talk is thinking in a realistic way that your brain can believe. You can throw positive thoughts at yourself all day long, but if they don't make sense, your brain will outsmart you and resort to negative thoughts that do make sense. Most negative thoughts are rooted in reality, or at least your brain's solid sense of reality. To counter them, you must think in positive ways that also make sense.

One way to make your brain believe what you are thinking is to create a SMART goal, a common mental hack used by athletes [6]. Tell yourself that you can accomplish something and then outline how you can so your brain actually believes you can do it. SMART stands for:

1. Is it specific? You must have a very clear idea of what your goal is in order to accomplish it. A

bad goal is "I want to become a better person" because you don't tell yourself what you really want to do. But a good goal is "I want to raise my income by ten percent to feel like a more accomplished person" or "I want to spend eight hours a week exercising to feel better about myself."

2. Is it measurable? Your goal must be measurable. For example, you want to get ten new contracts in a year. You must determine an actual number so that later you can evaluate your progress and see how close you are to the goal. If you are still far from your goal, you can work harder at it or set up new steps to make it more attainable. Also, you can use measurements to ascertain if your goal is realistic or if you should adjust it to make it more so.

3. Is it actionable? A goal must have specific and realistic actions that you can take to make it reality. You want to list action steps to reach your goal.

Breaking goals into smaller steps makes it seem more possible and less overwhelming.

4. Is it realistic? A goal that is not realistic will fail. Planning to become the richest man in America in one year is probably not realistic. Don't limit yourself but try to think of things that you can actually accomplish using the action steps you determined before.

5. Is it time bound? Your goal needs a deadline so you know when to complete steps to achieve it and you feel motivated to get things done. You might say that you want to acquire four new accounts in the next month at work, for instance. Having that timeline lets you measure the goal and see how many accounts you have acquired in a week, in two weeks, and finally in a month. You can see how close you are to the goal and how much more you must do to reach it by the deadline. Set a deadline for the ultimate goal and a timeline for each action

step to make it more achievable. Determine various milestones when you can step back and view your progress.

The Benefits Of Mindfulness Meditation

Mindfulness meditation is an incredible way to master your own mind and reprogram it [10]. Practicing it every day will teach you to focus on things more intently and stop thoughts before they gain any power over you. It is a great way to learn to still negative self-talk and redirect your mind to positive self-talk. The best part about it is that it is a conscious activity, so it helps your conscious mind stay on task and effectively reprogram your subconscious.

Buddha often talked about monkey mind, wherein your mind swings from thought to thought and mood to mood with little rhyme or reason. Negative self-talk and anxiety are often the products of monkey mind. Mindfulness helps you stop the swinging around and the intrusive negative thoughts that tend to come from monkey mind. This can lead to greater peace and inner harmony.

In fact, mindfulness meditation has been found to help patients overcome pain and it has positive implications in the healing of cancer patients [10]. This is because patients learn to focus on their feelings and then control them.

Mindfulness meditation has amazing effects, but it is not hard. Every day set aside five minutes to sit in silence, preferably in a peaceful place with no distractions. Focus on a spot on the wall and determine to look nowhere else. Begin to breathe in through your nose, out through your mouth. Concentrate solely on the act of breathing and looking at the spot on the wall. When you feel the urge to move or look away, resist it.

Intrusive thoughts will begin to cloud your mind.

Peacefully acknowledge a thought, then remind yourself to keep looking at the wall and breathing. This will redirect your thinking.

In time, you can increase the increments of time in which you meditate. You can also start to focus on tasks in the same way as you work, clean the house, do the dishes, or perform yard work. Even try it while you are driving and become a much better driver! With practice, mindfulness will become a habit that helps you stay focused and dismiss negative thoughts as they enter your mind.

Start to apply it to your thinking. When you are plagued by negative thoughts, worries, and doubts, you can dismiss those thoughts just as you do in meditation. You can then focus on something more positive. Mindfulness will help you gain the mental control and self-awareness that enables you to do this throughout the day, not just when you are meditating.

Neutralize Cognitive Distortions

Cognitive distortions are forms of negative thinking that distort reality negatively [5]. They can drive you to act in ways that are not helpful to your overall success. Neutralizing them involves writing down your thoughts, determining the applicable cognitive distortion, and then thinking in a new solution-oriented way to that restructures your view of reality and delivers results.

Rooted in cognitive behavioral therapy, this method helps you retrain your thinking over time. You learn to identify and stop poor thinking habits, or cognitive distortions, by replacing them with more helpful thinking. While you can use a therapist to accomplish this, you can also use a journal or workbook (many are available online for free or a small price) and do it yourself.

While there are many forms of cognitive distortions, the most common ones are as follows:

Black And White/All Or Nothing Thinking

This kind of thinking often underlies depression and jadedness. You assume that a person is all good or all bad. You think that by moving, life will become perfect. Then you are surprised and hurt when things don't turn out as black and white as you assumed. Life always has gray areas, a bit of good and bad mixed together. Understand this and you will find your emotions become much more stable.

Generalizations

When you generalize, you lump a person or situation into a broad category. You might generalize that all women are cheaters because one woman cheated on you, or you might assume that a person is bad because he reminds you of your father-in-law. You tend to make life negative when you make these broad generalizations. You may also limit yourself if you make a generalization about a person or job. Determine when you do this and decide to get more information before you make a judgment. Keep in mind that every person and situation is different.

Evaluations

You critique yourself against some sort of pre-determined standards. You may compare yourself to someone else or hold yourself to impossible expectations. You always fall short and this lowers your self-esteem. When you begin to compare yourself and measure yourself, write it down. Determine what you are making the comparison against. Then decide that comparisons are not helpful and you should just accept yourself for who you are and where you are in life. If you want to improve, decide where you can improve and how to do it. Use that determination to drive a SMART goal.

Blaming

You feel the need to assign blame to someone or to yourself for something that has gone wrong. You might accuse someone of messing up your life when you are the one who made a mistake. Or you might blame yourself for someone's death when you had nothing to do it with it at all. Write down thoughts in which you assign blame and then ask yourself what you actually did to cause the event in question, or what someone else did. Decide to focus on a solution instead of dwelling on anger and blaming others or yourself.

Assuming

When you assume, you make a decision that something you don't know is true. You might assume that someone hates you because he shot you a dirty look. You might assume that someone won't go out with you because he or she hasn't responded to your text for an hour. Operating on little information, you assume that something is true and then you act on it.

You may be mistaken. It is time to write down the things that you are thinking and determine if there is any basis for your assumption. If you don't have solid evidence for a decision, don't immediately make it.

Catastrophizing

This is where you make a mountain of a molehill. You assume that something is way worse or more disastrous than it really is. This thinking often drives anxiety and panic attacks. Write down something you are worried about. Decide if it really will hurt you as badly as you assume, or if it will turn out badly.

Give Yourself A Pep Talk

Most athletes have success using a self-pep talk to motivate themselves before an event [6]. Pep talks work by convincing your brain that you are able to do something. They build up your energy and self-esteem, creating the perfect recipe for success in your mind.

To give yourself a pep talk, you first must acknowledge the self-doubt that creeps into your thoughts. As you think these thoughts, calmly accept that you feel anxious or doubtful, and then tell yourself, "I want to feel motivated instead." Firmly turn your mind toward positive thoughts that build you up. Let the negative ones have their turn and then redirect your thinking to the motivating thoughts every time.

It is best to emulate someone who has given you encouraging pep talks before. You may think back to a coach, or a parent, or a teacher, or a best friend. Remember how the person spoke and how his or her words made you feel. Focus on that feeling and tell yourself similar encouraging things. You may also find a role model, such as a sports team coach, and watch him or her give a pep talk to learn how to structure yours.

Tell yourself that you can do something. Tell yourself that you have what it takes. And, finally, tell yourself that you will grow from this experience, no matter how you perform. It can be helpful to reflect on victories and triumphs you have had in the past.

Give yourself a pep talk anytime you feel nervous or doubtful about your abilities. You can do this before a job interview, a first date, a speech, or a big performance. You can do this when you're starting something new or taking on a big project that fills you with anxiety. Pep talks are especially helpful before big life events or changes when you feel most vulnerable to insecurities and doubt.

Achieve The Flow State

The flow state is an interesting state of calm deliberation and determination that martial artists, competitive athletes, and CEOs often utilize to get things done [11]. While the flow state leads to increase productivity, its true point is to learn to focus on the present to lead a happier life. Learning to exist in the flow state takes practice, which is optimized by using mindfulness meditation. Once it becomes habit, you will find that you have greater concentration, improved productivity, and better mental control that enables you to stop negative self-talk in its tracks.

When you are in the flow state, you are not letting anything distract you. You don't have room in your mind for insecurities. The results you are aiming for will drive you to work hard and they will boost your confidence.

Achieving the flow state is easiest when you are doing something you love because you are more willing to pour your entire heart into it. But it is more than possible to achieve it when you are taking on a daunting or tedious task. Challenges usually enable you to unlock the flow state.

- First, address your physical state. You must be

comfortable. You must not be hungry or tired. Physical discomfort will kill flow, so get comfortable before starting to ensure you don't suffer needless distractions from your own body.

- You must clear all distractions, including intrusive thoughts. Turn off your phone and choose to answer calls and emails at a later time. Make your space quiet so that you aren't distracted by noise. Ask other people to leave you alone.

- Spend a few moments meditating on a specific spot on the wall to clear your mind and gain laser focus. You must only look at that spot, as you breathe in through your nose and out through your mouth. You must treat thoughts and distractions as flies; you see them, you acknowledge them, but you don't chase them. Eventually, they will buzz away.

- Set a timer for 25 minutes. During those 25 minutes, you can only work on one thing. The more time you spend focusing on the task, the more your mind will clear and accept the task as your sole priority right now. You can allow distractions after the 25 minutes is up if you want, but chances are, your mind will become committed to seeing the task through all the way to the end during that time frame.

- Then, turn to your task at hand. Begin working on it and focusing on it. When intrusive thoughts enter your mind, calmly acknowledge them but don't chase them. Always turn your thoughts back to your work at hand. When a physical sensation distracts you, treat it in the same way.

Chapter 4: Self-Talk And Your Family

Thus far, you have learned how self-talk helps you. However, positive self-talk is not just beneficial for your own personal success. It can also lead you to achieve better relationships and better rapport with your family and friends. Your positive attitude and new aptitude for forgiveness can lessen tension. You show your family members more love. They become happier and learn to use positive self-talk from you. In turn, having a more peaceful and happy home life can improve your mood and carry over into other areas of life.

While many people claim to be good at compartmentalizing, the truth is that stress at home tends to negatively impact everything else in your life, from romance to work. You can become less confident if you are at odds with your family, which trickles into your work performance and your social life outside of the home. You also tend to feel stressed and suffer various subsequent physical and mental ailments. Obviously, these things will have a negative impact on the family unit, as well as all other areas of life.

Positive self-talk helps you show your family your good side. It helps you forgive grievances and build better communication to prevent future issues. Furthermore, it can make you feel better, so you are more able to treat your family kindly without taking out stress and unhappiness on them. Being confident and comfortable in your skin helps you overcome insecurities that you may inadvertently take out on your family. This can strengthen your relationships and improve the quality of your love.

Self-Talk To Improve Relationships With Your Family

We all have annoying habits, such as leaving toothpaste uncapped or littering socks across the bedroom floor. When you are trapped in the cycle of negative self-talk, however, you are under greater stress than normal. This can make you less forgiving about small annoyances, which in turn can make you act out aggressively against your family over small things.

Most people have said things they regret to their family members over remarkably trivial things; for example, it is not rare to take a bad day out on your family and explode over something like your spouse leaving the toilet lid up. These explosive and irritable behaviors can create negative feelings and strain between family members, which can cause bigger issues in the long run.

However, if you use positive self-talk, you can start to feel less stressed. That causes you to treat your family with less irritability and frustration. In addition, you should self-talk positively and out loud to your family over small issues, to show them what you are really feeling. They will be more receptive to your messages if you phrase them positively.

For instance, say you come home from a long day and your kids have left the house a total mess. Your normal reaction is to get angry and yell. Yelling only makes your kids feel defensive and even scared of your bad mood. It does not lead to a pleasant evening. Instead of yelling, you say out loud, „I don't like when you leave the house a mess because I step on Legos and it hurts. It is much safer to have a clean house. How about you guys help me pick up?"

As a result, your kids feel more eager to help you clean up. They also learn why you hate messes and why it is good to keep the house tidy. You also feel better because you don't harbor guilt for yelling or annoyance against your family. You don't build up negative emotions that make you cynical. You can simply relax with a tidy house and enjoy dinner with your kids and spouse.

Start by acknowledging when something your family

does annoys you. Look at it objectively using self-distance to see that this issue is not huge. Consider how you feel and how your mood may be influenced by other factors, such as stress at work or a long, exhausting commute. Decide not to take your mood out on your family, and instead let yourself feel grateful that you have a family to come home to. Focus on your feelings of love for your family members, letting it fill your heart and your mind.

When you have shifted into a more positive mood this way, you can think of a solution to the annoyance that triggered you in the first place that is not clouded by annoyance or anger. Think of how to positively word your feelings to your family that does not betray anger or any other bad emotions. Invite them to help you right the issue.

When using positive self-talk to your family, you want to always use positive phrases. You don't want to level accusations at your family members. Instead, say something like, "Let's work on this together." Provide suggestions for what each family member can do to improve the situation. Leave negative accusations and hurtful insults out of the talk.

You should also build communication by clearly stating how you feel. You don't want to do this in an emotional way. For instance, if stepping on a Lego makes you incredibly angry, take some time to neutralize the anger. Then tell your kids in a regular, calm tone that leaving Legos all over the floor makes you angry because it hurts when you step on them. You can then say, „Please pick them up."

Always use „I" messages to communicate what you are experiencing. Then use „we" phrases to help you invite collaboration with your family. For example, maybe your spouse drives you crazy when he or she puts the blender on first thing in the morning while you are trying to wake up. You may normally yell, „I'm trying to sleep!" but now you say, „I love getting my rest in the morning and I feel that I can't do that when you run the blender so early. Could we please run the blender after I get up?" You just used a combination of „I" and „we" messages to effectively communicate your feelings and a solution to the problem.

Finally, don't overload your family members with criticism. This only teaches your family to be critical of themselves and you; it creates a critical environment for everyone in the home and sets a poor model for how you treat each other. Avoid telling your family members about their flaws. Also, avoid saying things like, „You always do this!" or „You never do that!" Always and never are strong words and they are almost always exaggerations.

Never compare your family members to others. You might feel tempted to compare your youngest child, who is temperamental, to his calmer older sister. „I wish you were more like your sister!" This is an extremely critical and hurtful thing to say, as it teaches your child to always compare himself to others. In place of comparison, point out what the family member does that you like to make him or her want to do that more and make you happier. Back to the previous example, you could tell your youngest, „I loved the other night when you didn't throw a tantrum. How about we have another night like that?"

Consider when you want your spouse to do something romantic. You could say, „You never buy me flowers! Rene's husband always buys her flowers," which makes your spouse feel criticized and inadequate and less inclined to do what you want. Alternatively, you could say, „I loved that one time when you brought me flowers. I would love it if you did that more because it makes me feel good." Now your spouse feels praised for something good he or she once did, and he or she wants to do it more to get more praise. You didn't accuse him of anything and you didn't compare him to another person; you simply praised him for an action you want to encourage.

Positive reinforcement generally works better at getting the behavior you want than negative reinforcement [12]. As in the above example, you want to avoid accusations and phrases like always or never. Instead, praise your family member for behavior you like.

How To Avoid Taking Negativity Out On Family

It is common to take the stress of a traffic jam or a long day at work out on your family when you get home. The stress has built up in your over the course of the day, and you can't take it out on anyone at work without getting fired. Your family is an outlet for this stress. Unfortunately, your family deserves your best treatment and your love. Taking stress out on them when they aren't even the source of your stress is a bad way to keep their happiness and loyalty. Many couples get divorced because of this issue.

On your ride home from work, work on calming yourself and diffusing stress. Use mindfulness meditation as you drive to clear your head and focus purely on driving. Play some good music or a great audiobook to put you in an upbeat mood. Throughout the drive, use positive self-talk to also elevate your mood.

Reflect on what you did well during the day. Then praise yourself for that. This can make your day seem less stressful as you relish what you have accomplished. You should also tell yourself, "It was a hard day, but it helped me meet a few goals. I'm proud of myself. Good job!"

Before you pull into your driveway, be sure to reflect on how glad you are to come home. Look forward to seeing your family and relaxing with them. Don't focus on things like how your kids will start demanding your attention the minute you walk through the door or all of the chores you have waiting for you. This only makes you feel stressed before you walk through the door.

List three things you love about your family and three things you are grateful for before you walk through the door. Doing this helps you retain your positive attitude in the face of controversy or annoyance once you are actually around your family.

Maybe these steps don't apply to you because you are a stay-at-home parent or you work from home. Or maybe your stress lies in dealing with other family members who don't live with you and you must neutralize negative feelings before you have dinner with a toxic family member or go help your mother-in-law with a task you don't relish. The steps above can be modified to fit other scenarios. Take time to praise yourself for your hard work and dedication, reflect on things that you love about your family, and take some time to clear your mind of negative thoughts throughout the day or before spending time with family you don't particularly enjoy being around. Focus on the positive rewards of being around your family and how they have made your life better. Don't dwell on the things that you don't like.

If you are a stay-at-home parent, you should also ensure that you take some time to yourself at least once a week. Leave the kids with someone and go do something you enjoy. This preserves your sense of identity and helps you get over the stress of staying at home with the same people, day after day. Be sure to take a few moments out of each day to reflect on good things about your family so that negative feelings and frustration don't build up within you and leak out in your treatment of your family.

Teach Your Children Positive Self-Talk

I grew up in a very critical, negative environment. While my parents are both wonderful people, they tend to be hard on themselves. They also tend to compare and criticize me in a misguided attempt to make me the best version of myself. Growing up in this environment, my subconscious was programmed to be negative. I became an adult who believed that he didn't have the skills to be happy in life. It took a lot of work to overcome this attitude and adopt a healthier one.

The way you use self-talk transfers to your kids [13]. In a study comparing teachers who used positive and negative self-talk on their students, the outcomes showed much better grades and higher rates of self-esteem in students who heard positive self-talk in the classroom [13]. Children model themselves after the adults in their lives. You are a model for behavior to your kids, whether you realize it or not. Your behavior helps them form theirs. By using negative self-talk, you are setting a model for such negativity in your children. They will internalize this and start using negative self-talk themselves.

Many parents think that their bad habits will not transfer to their children as long as they hide these habits. For instance, you may use negative self-talk, but you speak positively to your children. That is great, but your children still see you using negative self-talk on yourself. Thus, they are still learning negative self-talk from you.

Don't let them grow up surrounded by negative thoughts and feelings. Set a better model by talking to yourself positively in front of them. When you make a mistake, tell yourself that you forgive yourself and then reason out a solution to teach them that all problems have solutions and self-forgiveness is possible. When you want to criticize yourself, focus on praising yourself instead to teach them to do the same. When you feel apprehensive or negative about something, speak optimistically out loud to teach them to always have a positive attitude.

By setting such a model for your children, you teach them to grow up and use positive self-talk on themselves. You also expose yourself to positive self-talk, which makes it more of a habit in time.

Always use your self-talk to model the way you talk to your kids. You want to speak to them the same way you want to speak to yourself. Don't compare or criticize them; simply encourage them and praise them for their positive attributes. When they are scared or anxious, uplift them with a pep talk. If you ever hear them speaking negatively, tell them how to rephrase that talk positively.

The way you talk to your spouse also influences how your kids grow up. You want to set a great model by always speaking to your spouse positively. Use constructive feedback instead of criticism, offer your spouse tons of praise, and focus on solutions to conflicts or problems as opposed to dwelling on the unhappiness of bad situations. Your marriage will improve, as will your kids' attitudes and future marriages.

Transfer Positivity To Your Spouse

An essential part of a good marriage is having continually positive interactions with your spouse. As you well know, marriage is not always happy. Stressful times and tense issues will inevitably arise throughout your relationship. However, the difference between couples who stay married and couples who get divorces tend to center around good conflict resolution skills.

Using positive self-talk can help you transfer positivity to your spouse. Your behavior will create a model for how your spouse feels toward you. Therefore, create a positive model. Your spouse will respond in kind.

Speak To Your Spouse Nicely

Creating a good model centers around speaking to yourself kindly. But you should also speak to your spouse kindly. Using the tips in the first section, speak to your spouse in a way that leaves out comparisons, accusations, and insults. Stop exaggerating your spouse's faults and focus on his or her good qualities. Communicate your feelings clearly with "I" messages and follow them up with "we" messages proposing collaborative solutions. Offer your spouse lots of positive reinforcement for behavior you want to encourage and politely ask for him or her to stop behaviors that bother you.

Focus On The Good Things

You should express lots of gratitude to your spouse. Always praise him or her for doing well. Tell him or her how grateful you are to know him or her.

Bringing home thoughtful gifts, even things as small

as your spouse's favorite candy bar or soda, is a great way to express gratitude and love. I like to bring my wife flowers "just because." This makes her feel appreciated and loved. In return, she likes to give me back rubs after a long day of sitting at my desk.

When your marriage hits a rough patch, you can calm the storm by taking time to reflect on the things you love about your spouse and the good parts of your marriage. This can help you stay positive and hopeful. It can motivate you to work through all the problems because the problems are worth the overall happiness you gain from the marriage.

Listen Impersonally

Listening is very imperative to any relationship. Sometimes, you may not want to hear something your spouse has to say. You may be faced with painful conversations. Listen to your spouse, nevertheless, and then take some time to meditate on his or her words.

Acknowledge negative emotions you may feel and then think of how you can feel more positively about the situation. Figure out how you can use the criticism constructively. Using CBT, analyze the situation when you take something personally to see if it is less of a big deal than you are making it out to be. You can always ask your spouse to clarify something or ask if he/she meant something hurtful. Your spouse can help you work through any negative emotions you may have about a conversation.

For example, when my wife claimed that I was being selfish by hogging the remote one night, I felt very hurt. Using my journal, I analyzed the situation and decided that I was probably assuming what she meant and catastrophizing the situation. I later asked her, "Did you mean that I'm a selfish person?" She clarified that she meant I was being selfish at that moment but that I'm a great person and she loves me.

I instantly felt better. We were able to overcome the issue.

Respect Boundaries And Needs

Respect your spouse's needs. There may be times when you infringe on your spouse's boundaries or fail to meet your spouse's expectations. Many people take their spouses' negative feedback far too personally and refuse to work on the issues at hand. This is a good way to alienate your spouse and break down your marriage.

If your wife complains about you making her uncomfortable when you speak to other women, for instance, you can use that to strengthen your relationship by changing your conversation toward other females. Be willing to change for your spouse.

Don't let anger and frustration build up when your spouse asks something of you. Instead, think of how you love your spouse and want to make him or her happy. Self-talk yourself into accepting your spouse's needs and not taking those needs as insults to your ego. Remember why you love him or her to convince yourself that changing yourself is worthwhile. A good marriage is founded upon a willingness to sacrifice certain activities or habits for your spouse's comfort and happiness.

Repel Pessimism

When your spouse is being negative or pessimistic, he or she can really lower your mood and feed your habit of negative self-talk. Always turn this around by responding positively. Teach your spouse to have a good attitude by having one yourself.

Say your spouse is anxious about an upcoming showcase and keeps talking down on herself. You can build her up with a pep talk and make her feel better. She will become happier and that will rub off on you. Essentially, you both create an equilibrium of positive emotions that nourish both of you.

Do Happy Things

Having a life apart from your spouse leads to a healthier relationship, as well. You tend to keep your independence and a sense of being your own person. You also have time away from your spouse, which helps you get over any irritation you may feel over little things. Have a hobby and friends outside of the marriage to blow off steam.

However, this does not mean that you should not spend time with your spouse. Your spouse should always be your number one priority. Becoming so obsessed with your new car that you fail to spend time with your wife is an example of how you can take a life outside of your marriage too far. You want to dedicate time to your spouse each day. Communicate that you love him or her via text message once a day when you are not together.

Doing things together outside of your normal routine can keep you both entertained and happy, as well. You should have mutual friends and activities or hobbies that you both enjoy doing together. Marriage counselors recommend for couples to have "date nights" where they court each other, just like before they got married. Dating can keep the romance alive and prevent your marriage from getting stagnant. A romantic dinner every now and then, a lovely vacation while the kids are in summer camp, and other such activities are good ways to date your spouse.

It is helpful to think of your marriage as a constantly evolving relationship. You must put in work to keep it from evolving into something sour or plain bad. You can keep the love alive through the same work you put in getting your spouse to fall in love with you.

Love at first is usually a trick of the memory [3].

There was actually a lot of work that went into the growth of your love for each other. Hence, always remember that feelings can change and are not permanent. You must continue to put in the same work to get the same results. Make some effort to keep the love alive through dates and your marriage will stay strong and happy.

Eliminate Jealousy And Insecurities

It is also key to build up your own confidence with self-talk. Often, you take things your spouse says too personally because of an insecurity you have that your spouse does not even know about. You may also feel insecure compared to others, so you become jealous and let jealousy fuel fights and distrust. Having confidence helps you overcome this.

For example, I had an insecurity about my lack of muscles for a long time. When my wife even looked at a male model on an ad or a show, I would feel a wave of resentment and jealousy. I was telling myself, "She probably wants someone who looks like that rather than me!" In time, I realized that I was the only one thinking this. I was letting my own insecurities about my body create a lot of strife and conflict with my wife when she loved me exactly for who I was. Therefore, I decided to work on my body satisfaction by going to the gym and repeatedly telling myself that I actually looked good. The result was less jealousy and more happiness with my wife.

With a happy family, you can have a better work life and more success in business. However, there are additional self-talk techniques and tricks to make your business stronger. Read on to learn how to enhance business with positive self-talk.

Chapter 5: Self-Talk For Business Success

What if I told you that you are your own worst enemy? It's not something you want to read, but it's true. Many people talk themselves out of success and happiness. Everyone has inner potential, but some people don't realize their potential due to insecurities or fear that they entertain inside their heads. They pass up on great opportunities and make excuses to avoid taking risks. The result is a life of failed and missed chances, stuck in a rut.

The key to your success really depends on you. By making a choice to take opportunities and live your best life, you make it possible. You can use positive self-talk to overcome fear and doubt. You can motivate yourself with intrinsically positive language.

When was the last time you felt excited about something? What was your thought process? Capture that moment in your mind and really experience it again. From now on, that same feeling is how you want to regard your business and your work life. Feel excited and imagine what could happen. Work to make things true, without letting doubt hold you back.

Make Impossible Tasks Possible

Find Solutions

People often assume that something is impossible. They find a dozen reasons to support this self-defeating belief, and those reasons are probably valid. You might think, "It will take forever to get my degree; I don't have that kind of time or money right now" or "I can't afford to launch my own business." But in reality, these "valid" reasons are just excuses. Instead of viewing these hurdles as challenges to overcome, you dwell on them and let them take control of your life. You give them far more power than they deserve. It is time to take that power back for yourself.

The science of motivation entails making the impossible possible. The very first (and perhaps most paramount) part of motivating yourself is removing the belief that something is impossible. You can do this by viewing all of the reasons why you *can't* accomplish something as simple hurdles to clear [14]. Basically, think of issues that may prevent you from something as a problem to be solved, rather than a wall blocking your progress.

I faced this when I wanted to go back to school. Without my degree, I had hit a dead end in my career. Plus, I really hated my job! Every job I wanted required a degree. I felt that life without a degree was impossible, but I also felt that obtaining my degree was impossible. So, I felt stuck and feeling stuck made me depressed. Then I realized that I was creating barriers around my mind, preventing myself from moving forward. Obviously, I wanted a degree, so what was stopping me?

First, I looked at the financial aspect. No, I didn't have the cash in hand to just pay my tuition and finish. But I knew there were ways to raise the money. I looked into financial aid and loans and made school possible.

Next, I considered the time barrier. Yes, it would take a few years, so I couldn't expect immediate results. And yes, not all of the coursework would be meaningful and fun. But I realized that if I at least did something, then the time commitment would be worth the end result.

Finally, I often used the logic "What if I don't get a job?" to limit myself. I realized that I was stopping myself from finishing college by focusing on a what-if scenario that may not even happen. Statistically, I knew people succeeded more with college degrees and earned more money. I decided to focus on that positive instead of the negative what-if.

Do you see what I did? I identified the biggest hurdles that made me assume something was impossible. Then I looked at them from different perspectives to find creative solutions to each problem. In the end, I was motivated enough to make my dream happen, and it all paid off.

Negative self-talk tells you that you can't do something. Positive self-talk says, "How can I do this?" You don't let anything get in the way. If there is a problem, you tell yourself that you can surmount it and you brainstorm how to go about doing that.

Gather Resources And Allies

Often, you dismiss an idea the minute a hurdle shows up. Now, you must think about the hurdle differently. Do things you never dared before – like asking people before you assume they will tell you no or looking into resources to help you get to where you want to go. You are not alone. Arm yourself with people and resources to make something happen. Research options and find out what is really out there. Never just assume "There is no way."

For example, my niece had some financial issues and her car was repossessed. For years, she couldn't get a loan, so she kept buying cheap cars that were on their last leg and dealing with expensive repairs. One day, she decided to take a different approach and actually talk to a bank and a car dealer to see if her financing options were truly as restricted by her past repossession as she had thought. While many lenders refused to lend to her, she actually managed to find one. Now she has a much safer and more reliable car. By talking to people and learning about her options, she was able to get rid of the assumption that she was stuck driving rattle traps forever.

Self-talk yourself into asking if there are options you have not explored. You probably have overlooked some possible resource or person who could help.

Now, look into how to make something happen. Just by taking this proactive approach, you start to build motivation and a sense that something is possible.

Are Your Barriers Even Real?

Consider if a barrier is truly real. In my case, I was dwelling on a what-if scenario, "What if I can't get a job?" There are always at least two possible outcomes to every scenario, either negative or positive. Choose to focus on the best possible outcome. It may not happen – but it may happen, too. If you don't try, you won't get to see the best possible outcome.

Try to stop catastrophizing possible bad outcomes, as well. You might assume that you will not make much money if you start your own freelance business. Well, is that really a horrible thing? We all know that money is essential to survival but taking a pay cut in exchange for a career that makes you happy is usually not going to end your life. Ask if a possible bad outcome will truly destroy your life or if you can survive it. Chances are, you can survive it, absolutely no problem.

Use Love To Drive Success

In a study, the main difference between students who feel motivated to study for math class and students who don't depends whether or not the student thinks he enjoys math [14]. When you do things you hate, you tend to feel no motivation. But when you do things you love, or at least work toward something you love, then you feel much more inclined to do it.

To make something possible, focus on what you love about your goal. Focus on how it will make you feel good and how it will improve your life. Use these thoughts as a motivational push toward success. You should write them down and post them somewhere you can see every day to keep your resolve strong.

There are two types of goals: mastery and

performance [14]. Mastery goals are when you feel determined to become competent at something. Performance goals are when you want to stack up to others and beat the competition. A study proved that performance goals tend to drive people to perform better on a test than those with mastery goals [14]. Therefore, you may find that setting a performance goal will motivate your success more because you tend to care more about what others think than how well you do at something.

So, if you are sad that you are not doing as well in life as your brother, use that to motivate yourself. You want to stack up or even beat your brother, and thus you do everything you can to accomplish that goal. Supposed character flaws, like competitiveness and sibling rivalry, can actually be very helpful.

Change your negative self-talk in this area. You should quit comparing yourself to others and feeling dismal that you don't stack up, thinking, "Everyone else is better than me!" Instead, you should think, "I want to do as well as this person I know, so I'm going to do it." Be positive when you use comparisons and evaluations.

Use A Mantra

Barriers to success are numerous. It makes you wonder how some people ever become successful. The true trick is to self-talk yourself that you can do anything. Recite the mantra "I can do this" at least three times. You should also recite this mantra whenever you feel like giving up.

Then write down what issues you are facing that block your success. For each issue, think of at least three solutions. Explore all of your options and write them down as well. This will break open so many doors for you.

Improve Your Interpersonal Relations

One day, your boss calls you into his office and berates you for a mistake. You feel horrible and you go home in a depressed mood. You think about how you hate your boss and your job and you want to quit. And you feel that you can't do anything right.

This negative self-talk at play, breaking down the quality of your relationships at work. You let your inner voice get to you, convincing you that everything is horrible and you hate everyone in the office. Your self-esteem suffers even more than it has to about making a human mistake.

You can change your self-talk to build up your relationships and your self-esteem at work. Use positive self-talk to recover from the ego blows that conflicts at work deliver.

Don't Take Things Personally

When your boss berates you at work, he or she is not insulting you as a person. Your boss views you as an employee and values your quality of work. When you goof, his or her reaction is toward your work, not you as a person. This is where personal and professional realms tend to conflict. You feel like a terrible person, but your boss is not saying that. You must make the distinction between personal and professional in your mind with positive self-talk.

Many people view work as a source of ego [15]. They draw pride from successes, and they suffer humiliation from failures. This makes their personal and professional lives overlap in a negative way. Remove the ego from your work. Remember that work is about your performance for a company, not your own personality. You are valued purely on what you bring to the table. Therefore, don't take setbacks or criticism as personal insults. Instead, take them as pointers on how to hone your work to fit the company's needs and become a more valued worker.

You can also stand out to your boss by requesting constructive criticism. Ask him or her, "What can I do better?" He or she will appreciate this rare yet noble bid for self-improvement.

Rely On Yourself

To succeed at work, you must trust that you are capable of succeeding. You must rely on yourself and trust your abilities to get things done. No goal or task can be too big for you.

Look for things you can contribute. Volunteer yourself for activities or tasks you are capable of doing. By showing your confidence to others, you inspire them to have confidence in you. This can raise you to the top of your team.

You should give yourself pep talks. "I can do this." "I

have what it takes." Saying things over and over convinces you that they are true. Then you act accordingly.

Speak Positively To Your Co-Workers

Just like how you can transfer positivity to your spouse to make him or her more positive, you can transfer positivity to your co-workers. Your co-workers will find your positive attitude appealing and will follow suit with their own behavior.

Start by always presenting praise and compliments to your co-workers to make them like you more. Smile more, too. Being pleasant to be around will make you fit in better at work.

You should learn to phrase criticism tactfully. You don't want to tell someone, "You are wrong" or "You are horrible at this!" or "You did the worst job I've ever seen." You want to say something more like, "I can appreciate what you have done, but I see room for improvement." Then offer tangible ways the co-worker can improve.

Don't take bad moods or stress out on your co-workers. Breathe through emotions instead of yelling or snapping at others.

Project a can-do attitude by always inviting others to help you find solutions. You can build up everyone's morale when you encourage everyone to work together to overcome a setback or hurdle. Pep talk yourself and everyone else by saying, "We can do this! We just have to pull together and make it happen!"

Invite Teamwork And Collaboration

You've probably seen those motivational posters, saying lame things like "Teamwork makes the dream work!" But these posters are not wrong. To truly improve the quality of your work relationships, you must inspire a sense of collaboration and cooperation between yourself and everyone else in the office.

Remember in Chapter 4, when I covered inviting collaboration with your family using "we" phrases? This approach to communication is even more essential in the work atmosphere. You want to invite collaboration to fix problems and meet goals with all of your co-workers. An organization is like an ecosystem, where every member contributes something to the overall goal. When one member is left out or not utilized, the whole team suffers from the lack of value that that one person can add to the work being performed. Hence, you must include everyone.

There is always that one person in the office who seems lazy and/or incompetent. Often, these people are simply unmotivated to rise to their potential. Including them in the team can motivate them. In turn, that motives you more. You should find the specific strengths that this person has and assign that person a task that uses those strengths.

When You Don't Like A Co-Worker

Just like you shouldn't take things said at work too personally, you should not base your interactions with your team on personal feelings, such as dislike. This is obviously easier said than done. Some people in the office just don't behave like adults, while others have completely communication styles and work preferences than you which can make working together extremely difficult.

To get over the sense that you don't like someone, focus on the person's positive attributes and strengths. Build the person up in your mind. As you treat this person more positively, his or her treatment of you will likely improve.

Improve communication by changing your style.

People communicate using modalities [16]. One person might process information visually, so he communicates in a visual way, saying things like "Do you see what I see?" or "Picture this!" But his communication is lost on the co-worker who uses an auditory modality and processes auditory information better, and who prefers to say things "Do you hear what I'm saying?" or "Listen to this idea!" The two can find common ground by modifying their modalities. The guy who is more visual would be wise to avoid using graphs and flow charts in a presentation to the lady who uses an auditory modality; the lady with the auditory modality would benefit by communicating to her co-worker using pictures or PowerPoints.

To improve relations with someone who is hard to work with, you should adjust your modality. Miscommunication and annoying mishaps can be avoided thusly. You may think, "Why should I be the one to change? Why doesn't anyone try to adjust their modality for me?" Well, other people have not read this book. You can be the bigger person and make a positive difference at work by taking responsibility for your actions through the knowledge you have obtained in these pages. Your self-esteem will soar when you are the one to trigger positive changes at work.

Realistically, you won't get along with every person and sometimes you will have conflicts with co-workers you normally get along with. It is common to have at least one co-worker who acts like a petulant child and spreads gossip, as well. You can use a stress-diffusing self-talk technique when a co-worker starts to get under your skin.

First, take a quick break, such as a bathroom break. Spend some time sitting in silence. Close your eyes and focus on the in and out of your breathing. Tell yourself, When I open my eyes, I will no longer feel mad. Wait a few moments and then open your eyes. The irritated feeling should vanish. Now go back to work and focus on your task, rather than the person who is angering you. When you start to feel irritated again, redirect your thoughts back to your task at hand to regain concentration on the right thing.

Be Assertive

One of the only ways to get by around people is to use assertive language [17]. Assertive language is not rude or aggressive. It is not passive or manipulative, either. You simply state what you want and stand by it.

Assertively set boundaries at work. Let people know what you expect and what you don't tolerate. Using "I" messages, communicate things in clear terms. Don't let anger or insults seep into your words. Speak levelly and firmly, while holding eye contact. Be sure to be polite and use phrases like "please." After you ask someone to do something, say "Thank you" as if they have already done it. This motivates people to complete what you ask of them without argument.

A lot of issues with your relationships at work can be eradicated by setting boundaries. People know what is wrong – but they like to test boundaries and see what they can get away with. By setting and standing behind your boundaries, you can easily gain the respect of others. You may fear that people will get mad at you, but it is more likely that they will gain healthy respect for you when you stand up for yourself.

Gain Self-Motivation For Tedious Tasks

Every job has its fun, interesting aspects...and it's not-so-fun aspects. The tedious or challenging parts of our jobs may not be fun, but they are part of the day-to-day. You must get used to such tasks and you must learn to get them done if you want to be successful.

Don't assume that every rich CEO spent every day of

his life sipping coffee in front of his awesome view of the city. He was probably once a paper pusher, and later he was in middle management, doing things he hated. Now he is still forced to make hard decisions, endure boring meetings, and handle rejections and losses. You may envy somebody, but never assume that any other person has it all. Everybody has challenges and boring or unpleasant moments at work.

You should pinpoint the parts of your job that you don't like very much. What do you always put off until the last minute? Maybe you are not much of a phone person so you procrastinate phone calls and call in sick for conference calls. Maybe you hate doing paperwork, so you let it accumulate in a big stack until it becomes truly overwhelming. Maybe the act of going through documents with a fine-toothed comb gives you a headache so you dread it until you have no choice but to do it. Write down precisely what you hate about your job and what you tend to procrastinate.

Now, explore the reasons why you hate these particular tasks. What do they make you feel? Are you afraid of failure, or of public speaking? Are you not good at math? These reasons are all challenges to overcome. If you are bad at math, for instance, you can take a refresher course to help you handle the mathematical aspect of your job. Make the reasons you hate certain parts of your work disappear so that you can accomplish them.

Create A System

The most helpful part of motivation is creating a system. Systems are smooth routines that you follow to accomplish certain tasks; they automate the process for your brain. You can start your work day with something you hate, such as paperwork. Get it over with and consider how great you'll feel without a looming stack of papers to fill out at the end of the day. Once the paperwork is over with, you can shift to things you like more about your job.

For instance, I know several social workers. Often, paperwork is the thing they hate most about their otherwise rewarding careers. Most social workers have overcome this hatred by having a system in place to get paperwork done. For five minutes after a meeting with a client, they dedicate themselves to filling out paperwork. If they have to move on to something else, they leave themselves sticky notes for what to finish. Then they finish the paperwork in spare moments before they treat themselves to lunch or a break. They do this to automate the process they hate so much so that they don't procrastinate.

Reward Yourself

Always reward yourself after you complete a task. Doing it right before lunch or a break is a good way to motivate yourself because you know you will enjoy your free time so much more without the looming thought of the task you dread on your mind.

Always tell yourself, "You did a good job!" when you complete an arduous or unpleasant task. Your brain will respond to this message with a flood of feel-good serotonin. In the future, it will feel more motivated because it anticipates that rush of serotonin again. Tell yourself what a good worker you are and how well you did to reward yourself.

Work In The Flow State

Achieving the flow state also helps you with challenging aspects of work. Clear your mind with meditation, reduce distractions, and set a timer for 25 minutes. Then throw yourself into the dreaded task at hand. At the end of 25 minutes, you can move on to something else, but you'll probably want to see the task through to completion.

Break Tasks Down Into Steps

A task seems overwhelming when you view it in its entirety. But when you break it down into bite-sized chunks, your brain sees how it can accomplish the said task. It can then figure out how to tackle the task, bit by bit until it is completed. In fact, studies have indicated that there is increased brain activation and thus better performance when you use subtasks while driving [18].

First, look at the ultimate goal. Then, establish the subtasks that will accomplish that goal. Say your goal is to finish your taxes. You start by gathering documents together, then by signing into your tax account, then by filling out the first page, and so on.

Make a checklist on a piece of paper or in your phone. There are great checklist apps for your phone. Write down the main task and then list subtasks under it. After you complete each subtask, check it off and take a moment to tell yourself, "Great job! Now you're one step closer." This is positive encouragement to keep going until you can check the whole task off. You can also measure your progress, which is essential to every SMART goal. As you see yourself getting closer and closer to completion, you will feel more victorious and motivated to carry on.

Have A Life Outside Of Work

I love what Jennifer Aniston's character in *Office Space* said to the main character: "Lots of people hate their jobs. But they find something that they enjoy." It is true that if you hate your job, you can balance that negativity out with activities that you love outside of work.

Spending too much at work can burn anyone out. You need to get away and stop thinking about work for a while. As you go home, redirect your thoughts to things other than work. Leave work at work, in other words. When you are lying in bed at night and you start ruminating on a project you have to do tomorrow, clear your mind with a quick, silent mindfulness meditation.

Be sure to have a hobby, exercise class, fun club, or something else to do that has nothing to do with work. Spending time around other people and not thinking about work can refresh you and reset your brain for the next workday. You no longer feel as if your life is work because your life contains many other elements.

Does this mean that you should tolerate a job that withers your very soul? Absolutely not. I didn't, and I'm so much happier as a result. If you positively hate everything about your job, take some time to yourself to see if your interest in it renews. If time away doesn't help, then you need to focus on finding a new job. Let the hatred you feel for your job be your motivation to find something better. Tell yourself, "I deserve to be happy" and then coax yourself to abandon fear to find a new job.

Win That Promotion

You work hard for a promotion, and it goes to someone else. You think "Next time" and keep working hard. Then someone else gets the laurels once again. Now, you feel bitter and you think, "My boss just doesn't like me. Good things only happen to other people."

Remember, what you think is what you are. If you take a defeated approach to life, you will be defeated in life. The real success is in believing in yourself and staving off the bitterness that getting passed over can bring.

You can start by self-talking yourself into believing that you are worthy of that promotion. If you believe that a promotion is an attainable goal, then you will be more inclined to work hard to achieve it.

If you get passed over, don't take it as a personal reflection of who you are as a person. Think, "I deserved that but I didn't get it. How can I improve myself to get it next time?"

You should use rejections constructively. That way, you can improve your performance to get the recognition you deserve.

Sometimes, you may be a great worker and a valuable asset to the company, but you don't do anything to get your boss's attention. Of course, you will be passed over if you don't stand out. Often, the people who speak the loudest are the only ones who are heard. To gain attention at work, start to speak up. Let your boss know you want a promotion and why you deserve it. Volunteer ideas out loud and think creatively to stand out from the crowd. Do things a bit differently to get your boss's notice.

When you do something, be sure to point it out to your boss. You may feel embarrassed to promote yourself so blatantly, but the people who get promotions and raises tend to be the biggest self-promoters. American culture does not reward shyness or modesty; letting people know what you have done well is often the only way to gain their admiration and respect. So, the next time you land a huge account, announce it to your boss proudly.

Ask your boss for some time. Then present to him or her your greatest achievements and accomplishments and skills. Point out how you can use them in a new position. You may also point out strengths you have that your current position does not require, to illustrate how you can contribute even more from a new position. Afterward, thank your boss for his or her time. This ingratiates you with your boss by making you look respectful and polite. Urge your boss to think about promoting you before you leave the office.

If your boss tells you no, ask why. Then use his or her words constructively. Perhaps your boss doesn't think you have what it takes. Now you can tell yourself, "Let's prove him/her wrong!" Perhaps your boss thinks that someone else is better suited for the job. Tell yourself, "I will use this competition to prove myself."

In some cases, the cards are not stacked fairly in your favor. Maybe your boss is unprofessional and doesn't like you. Or maybe your boss promotes his family instead of non-family workers. In such a toxic work environment, you may not ever be able to win. You should remind yourself that you are worth more and seek a job that actually values your contributions.

With self-talk at work, you can enjoy much more success. But work and family are not the only areas of life that can benefit from self-talk. Read the next chapter to learn how to begin using self-talk to enrich your social life and make better friends.

Chapter 6: Positive Self-Talk For Social Relations

When I began using positive self-talk, I noticed a huge change in my social life. Not only did I make friends more easily, but my friendships tended to be better quality than before. While I believed that I had good social skills before I started using positive self-talk, I later realized that my negativity was hurting my friendships and attracting the wrong types of people into my life.

Part of my self-talk training included a book entitled *Safe People: How to Find Relationships that are Good and Avoid Those That Aren't*. In this book, I learned that certain people kept me trapped my cycle of negativity and reinforced my toxic beliefs by being negative themselves. I learned to be more discerning about the people I allowed into my life by evaluating if people are safe or not. The book also taught me to believe that I was worthy of safe people.

Self-talk is important for your social life. It makes you more upbeat, which draws more people into your life. It helps you overcome difficulties that hold you back from a rich social life, such as shyness. Finally, it teaches you to believe that you are worthy of good people who treat you well. You are more able to identify toxic people and eliminate them from your life because you know that you deserve better.

As you get to know more people with whom you have quality relationships, your confidence will soar. The fact that people like you will make you like yourself more. You will find more opportunities in life and work. Last but not least, you will have allies to help you through life's trials and tribulations. A good social life is inherent to success, so you should start using self-talk to enhance your social life immediately.

Overcoming Shyness With Self-Talk

Shyness can be the number one thing holding you

back when it comes to your social life. You fail to talk to people, so no one gets to know you. You are forgotten when people throw parties or pick team members because no one really knows you. Dating can be a special kind of nightmare for shy people, as well.

Overcoming shyness is the subject of numerous books and articles. But really, it boils down to one thing: using self-talk to increase your social skills. Since what you think makes who you are, it makes sense that believing you are shy makes you shy. Believing that you are actually outgoing and comfortable around people makes you outgoing and comfortable around people.

Imagine yourself as brave, calm, extroverted, and fearless. Take a few moments to meditate on this feeling. Visualize clearly how you feel in a social situation. The sweaty palms and shakes that you normally feel don't exist in your visualization; you feel totally cool and smooth. Now, imagine what you say to people. Imagine having great conversations and walking out of a party with a stack of business cards from people who really want to get to know you more. Let yourself feel this experience as if it were really happening.

This visualization helps tell your brain what is possible and how to act. But visualizations only go so far. To actually reap the benefits of self-talk for shyness, you need to apply self-talk in real life.

Start by signing up for some social event. It could be a party, or a Meetup, or a networking event. Normally, these events fill you with dread. Using self-talk, repeat the mantra: "I am an outgoing person who will make friends." Focus on how excited you are to meet new people and view this as a chance to make new connections. Remind yourself that your ego does not hinge on what others think of you so that the event becomes less critical and daunting.

During the event, smile and walk tall and straight. Your posture will influence your confidence and the way others see you [20]. Make the first move by going up to people and saying hi, offering a firm handshake. The more people you talk to, the more you will feel outgoing. Be sure to speak in a strong voice at a volume that is ideal for the situation you are in. People will soft voices tend to be overlooked [21]. Several studies have shown that women who speak in louder, deeper voices tend to be taken more seriously and men with deeper, louder voices are more attractive to women [21]. Hence, you want your voice to be fairly deep and loud to make people notice you, whether you are female or male.

Be picky. As you meet new people, evaluate how they treat you and how they treat others. An unsafe person will try to get favors or personal information out of you [19]. They will probably seem very trustworthy and charming, but their motives are likely bad. People who seem warm and caring, who don't ask for personal details, or who appear shy are likely safer people [19]. Listen to your gut on this. Don't pursue relationships with unsafe people.

Doing this helps remove some of the pain that may limit you in social relationships. Chances are, you are used to social rejection and you feel inadequate because of how people treat you. Now, you can dismiss such people as "unsafe" and believe that you are worthy of better treatment [19]. The result is that you walk away from social events with far less stress and misery.

Be sure to analyze your reactions to people. Are you taking what someone said too personally? Are you engaging in comparisons, fueling your jealousy and sense of inadequacy? Are you using black and white thinking, assuming that everyone is all bad or all good? Write down negative thoughts about the social event afterward and see if you are employing any cognitive distortions.

Self-Talk For Better Communication

Before I started doing personal work on myself, I was often nervous about speaking to others. I would stutter as I tried to think of the right thing to say. I would stop talking when people turned and spoke to each other, my thoughts grinding to a screeching halt. And I would talk only about what others wanted because I was scared that starting my own line of conversation would be met with rejection.

In time, I learned that people liked me more when I dominated the conversation and spoke clearly. If I didn't stop speaking and I didn't stutter, people would pay attention. If I told a story or joke, people would listen and even laugh and a whole new conversation would start around the subject of my story or joke. My conversations improved when I started acting like a conversational powerhouse.

One way to achieve this is to speak in front of a mirror. Rehearse a story that you have in mind to generate laughs or open up new topics. Think of interesting facts or current events to bring up. If you speak first and introduce a great conversational topic, people will be more eager to speak with you. Make sure that what you say is positive, however. Complaining will only put people off. But if you praise something, comment on how nice an event is, or give someone a compliment, you can spark a much more engaging and upbeat conversation that other people actually want to take part in with you.

Another way is to visualize yourself as a great speaker. You want to envision yourself possessing eloquence and aplomb. Imagine standing before an audience, delivering a speech to great applause.

Start to practice conversations on strangers in public places. For instance, tell your barista that her hair looks nice and then bring up the latest events in the city as she makes your coffee. Or tell a stranger on the bus a joke. While strangers may not want to talk to you, attempting to initiate conversations with them can teach you how to do so in a more effective manner. You will get more comfortable, especially when you realize that people respond to you positively if you speak to them positively. Plus, the likelihood of seeing this stranger again is slim, so you don't have to worry about being humiliated in front of someone you know.

Now move up to a co-worker you barely speak to or someone you want to get to know. Try to spark a relationship by starting a conversation or offering a compliment. As you see people respond, your confidence will grow yet more.

With this practice, you are readier to take on conversations with people who make you nervous. You also feel more at ease in dense social situations, where you must compete with other people to dominate the conversation and hold someone's attention. The good thing about denser social situations is that you don't have to take it personally when someone stops listening to you in order to listen to someone else. This is just the way of parties and group conversations. Keep inserting yourself in the conversation and be flexible to new topics that others bring up so that you stay relevant in the group. Be sure to speak loudly so people hear you over the din of dozens or hundreds of voices. Keep talking when someone interrupts you to assert your dominance.

Self-Talk To Improve Self-Esteem

Obviously, people value confidence. Having higher self-esteem tends to enhance your success in social situations and that social success enhances your success in life in general. According to numerous studies, most people find confidence very attractive [22].

Perhaps you are not a confident person. Or you are

confident, but you tend to lose your confidence in new situations. While both circumstances are normal, they are certainly problematic.

Start by practicing self-love and self-care. As you love yourself, you tend to feel better about yourself. Working on your cognitive distortions also tends to make you view life in a better light, which increases your confidence. Also, holding a strong, confident posture tends to influence how you feel about yourself and how others perceive you [20].

To build confidence, think back on your greater triumphs. From taking home a blue ribbon at a science fair in the seventh grade to winning a promotion at work, you have undoubtedly accomplished at least a few great things in your life. Always think of them when you feel insecure to remind yourself of how awesome you can be.

Also, recite what you are capable of. Maybe you are

not a very confident person, but one night you were and you did very well at a convention. Think back on that night and how you accomplished that sense of being on top of the world. Tell yourself that since you have done it before, you can certainly do it again. Hold the feeling of your accomplishment in your mind and relish it, letting it fill you. Desire to experience that again.

Before a situation where you normally feel insecure, recite the mantra, "No mountain is too high." Visualize yourself as a tall, strong person who is capable of great feats. Doing these two things reprograms your mind to think of you as a more confident person. As a result, your confidence skyrockets.

After any situation where you were insecure, write down what happened. Why do you feel insecure? Perhaps you embarrassed yourself; remember that most people are more concerned with themselves than you so probably no one even noticed your embarrassment, or they will forget it by tomorrow. Perhaps you felt rebuffed; remind yourself that you are catastrophizing the situation and you were probably not really rebuffed. Try to think of at least three things you did well during the situation that you want to do again, as well.

A large source of insecurity stems from your body image. If you feel fat, unfit, or somehow unattractive, you tend to suffer socially because people can tell that you are insecure. Before any social situation, look at some flattering photos of yourself or look at yourself in the mirror. Tell yourself how beautiful you are and how your body is a miracle. If you still feel insecure, try to dress, fix your hair, or apply makeup in a flattering way to make yourself feel beautiful. Wearing nice clothes (and nice underwear) alone can make you more confident.

Don't search for confirmations of your insecurities in

others. Many people do this as a habit. Perhaps someone makes a fat joke and you take that as a personal insult to your weight; perhaps someone states that he doesn't like women with red hair and you're insecure about being a redhead. Remember that people's opinions have little bearing on your actual life. For each person who doesn't care for how you look, there is probably someone out there who does.

Furthermore, people seldom mean anything personal when they throw out such negative opinions. They are simply negative, judgmental people who make shallow rules about the kinds of people they like based on looks. It is safe to dismiss and ignore these people in favor of people who don't make such comments. Chances are, the person who made a fat joke did not intend for it to hurt you, but he clearly lacks manners. The person who commented on how unsavory redheads are is limiting his social life by basing his choices in women on something as superficial and temporary as hair color. Neither of these people probably meant to attack you personally. They probably did not even know that you harbor insecurities about the things they brought up. They are simply rude, and you should brush their comments off. Refuse to take these opinions as confirmation that something is wrong with you.

If you are still dating, you can apply these tips to asking someone out and making a good impression on a date. But there are a few extra steps that apply to dating. Read on to make your love life amazing.

Chapter 7: Positive Self-Talk For Your Love Life

Your love life can drastically improve as you use self-talk. By building your confidence, you become a more attractive prospect. You also have fewer qualms about asking people out. You are willing to set boundaries and high standards because you know you are worthy of the best. Additionally, you never let shyness hold you back as you go after what you want, always working toward a big end goal.

Ultimately, the same skills you use for your social life will work for your dating life. Playing the dating game is very similar to making new friends. You must project confidence, speak well, and be charming to make a good impression. The goal may be different, but you will be doing many of the same things.

Grow Your Self-Esteem And Improve Your Body Image

Women rate men as more attractive based on their confidence [22]. Men also rate women as more attractive on this scale and continually state that insecure women are turn-offs. Having high self-esteem is essential to handle the rejection and pain that can arise in dating.

Dating can often feel as nerve-wracking as a job interview. You must make a good impression and even then, you still may not stack up to the competition. Therefore, you want to solidify the belief that you are absolutely worthy of winning first place in someone's heart. You must strive to accept yourself for who you are, so that you find the right partner who actually cares for you.

Love at first sight is typically just a trick of the memory [3]. Hence, no one will just love you on the first date. Nor will you fall in love with someone on the first date. Get rid of that idea. The true purpose of a first date is to establish yourself as someone worth getting to know, or in other words, making a good first impression. You can't do this if you talk down on yourself, behave nervously, or speak little because you are ashamed of yourself.

First, you want to look your best. Looking good enhances your confidence, but it also gives the impression that you actually care about yourself. This is a huge plus on any first date. Dress to impress!

Second, self-promote yourself. You don't want to hang back in modesty since modesty never pays out for anyone. Point out what makes you a great person. Mention your accomplishments and some cool things you have done in your lifetime. Talk about your positive attitude.

Third, always speak positively about yourself. Now is not the time to criticize yourself or mention your flaws. As you talk about yourself, use lots of positive words and upbeat language. Point out the good that came out of bad situations to prove that you have a good outlook on life. Seek silver linings in everything. For instance, if your dinner arrives burnt, make light of it and find a silver lining in the fact that you get a free meal out of the situation.

Finally, don't focus on yourself overly much. You want to talk about yourself a little bit to let the other person know who you are. But follow each statement about yourself with a question like, "What about you?" This invites the other person to speak about himself or herself. It helps you deflect attention away from yourself, so you don't dwell on your insecurities. By pouring all of your focus into listening to what the other person says, you can come up with relevant responses that keep the conversation going. Your attention will be very flattering to your date.

Before going on a date or asking someone out, give yourself a pep talk. Remind yourself how great you are. That confidence will show through when you make an impression on someone else. You can then have the self-love to sell yourself by telling this person how much you like him or her and how you can offer a great date.

Nothing repels dates faster than a bitter attitude or an attitude that you are not worthy. Think that you are worthy of the best. Don't let your thoughts drift to past rejections or bad dates or your ex; redirect them to the present when they do. When you talk to your new date, don't bring these things up. Focus on the positives in your life to lighten the mood.

Get Someone's Attention

Having more confidence helps you get someone's attention. This is because you fearlessly promote yourself and demand his or her notice. You won't get passed over or rejected as much if you actually put yourself out there and make your crush notice you.

Move elegantly. Walk with a confident posture and try to make yourself taller with a straight spine or even taller shoes. The result is that people notice you more. Don't cross your legs or arms, sit turned away from someone, or point toward an exit, as these things can subconsciously close yourself off to someone. Instead, face him or her head-on and keep your body language open.

Also, wear red. Red tends to be the color of sex [23]. Even just a dash of red, such as red lipstick or a red flower in your hair or a red tie, can make the opposite sex notice you more.

When you speak, speak eloquently. Enunciate clearly and speak in a volume everyone can hear. Propose a conversational topic to initiate communication. Then stimulate flow by listening well and replying to a person's words with a relevant topic. Balance listening with talking, devoting about fifty percent of your conversation to each.

The ideal way to get someone's attention is to stand out from the crowd. You can accomplish this by observing someone and learning what he or she likes. Say you have noticed a girl in your favorite coffee joint, always sipping on the same kind of latte. The next time you see her, smile and offer to buy her the latte she likes. This will certainly make her notice you.

Commenting on what someone is wearing and pointing out similarities can also help you gain attention by stimulating a friendship-based neural response [24]. Say a guy is wearing a Dolphins jersey and you grew up in Miami. You can get his attention by telling him that you're a Dolphin yourself or that you went to a game once. Or say a girl is reading a book you read once. Say, "Good book! I love [insert author's name]." Doing this creates a point of common interest that instantly stimulates someone's dopamine receptors, causing him or her to feel good and want to talk to you more [24].

A final great way to come up with a fantastic opener. This could be a corny pickup line to make someone chuckle. Or you could tell a joke. This approach is risky because someone may not respond to your opener well. But you know that you need to take risks to make life happen. Therefore, come up with some clever attention-getting openers. Your goal is to make someone aware of your existence. Saying something unusual (but not terrifying) will accomplish this goal. From there, you have the person's attention long enough to make a good impression and possibly get a date.

Tell yourself that you can accomplish all of this. Rehearse it in front of a mirror. Visualize how your date will go and emphasize positivity in the visualization. These steps will help you calm your nerves and act more becomingly during the date.

Gain practice by talking to people toward whom you feel neutral. Polishing your social skills with practice can make you more confident when it comes to talking to a person you like, which obviously tends to make you more nervous.

Also, don't blow the situation up in your mind to be bigger than it is. Humans tend to put the people they like on a pedestal and then base their ego on whether or not those people like them back. You can lessen the anxiety that comes with talking to people you find attractive by downplaying the situation in your mind. Tell yourself that this is just a conversation with a potential friend, not a potential spouse. Tell yourself, "If this person doesn't want to be with me, that's not a reflection of who I am. It is a reflection of who they are and where they are in life. I can find someone else who is ready for me." If you do get rejected, repeat this as a mantra to lessen the hurt. Think, "His/her loss."

Chapter 8: Growing Positive Self-Talk As A Habit

In Chapter 2, I talked about how self-talk works and in Chapter 3, I talked about how you can attain it by reprogramming your subconscious with your conscious. While I covered several techniques in that chapter that can help you gain control over your own mind and reprogram your subconscious, I want to touch on a few more now that you can use every day to make positive self-talk a habit. These simple steps can be combined with Chapter 3 to increase your positive self-talk use and eliminate negative self-talk.

Remember, negative self-talk is a habit that you can work to replace with the habit of positive self-talk. Through time and effort, you can change your whole way of thinking. Don't fall into the trap of believing that you can't control your own mind and change your habits just because you have been trapped in the cycle of negative thinking your whole life, you were raised in a negative environment, and/or you have been through some incredibly bad things in life. If I could do it, then so can you. I was raised around negativity and engaged in negative self-talk for most of my adult life, before acquiring positive self-talk through great introspection and personal work. I know that you can do it and see amazing results throughout your entire life.

But you can't wait. You must start today and begin to dedicate yourself to this work. As it takes time to make positive self-talk a habit, you must start sooner than later so that you can achieve your desired results sooner than later.

Power Of Positive Affirmations

Positive affirmations work stunningly well in cementing habits [24]. By repeating an affirmation to yourself over and over, you tend to make your mind believe it. Your mind will think of your positive affirmation automatically whenever you encounter an applicable situation simply because you have created neural pathways within the brain for the affirmation.

Positive affirmations are short phrases that trigger a helpful or positive feeling and image within your mind. By saying an easy-to-remember phrase or even a single word that means a lot to you, you can overcome many things. You can breed such desirable traits within yourself as positive thinking, optimism, confidence, problem-solving, self-efficacy, and gratitude. All of these traits will make you feel better about yourself and about your life.

You want to repeat your positive affirmation at least three times a day. You should also repeat them when you are facing a situation that tests your confidence or patience. The affirmation will only work if you use it. Cement it by using it throughout the day, and then gain from it by using it in trying circumstances when you really need a boost in confidence or positivity.

A good positive affirmation is something that you

identify with. You can think of your own, or you can try one that therapists recommend. Here are a few examples of great positive affirmations to repeat to yourself throughout the day.

- "I know and accept myself."
- "I believe that I can do this."
- "I trust my gut."
- "I have everything it takes to get this done."
- "I will see this through to the end."
- "I always persevere."
- "I forgive myself for my mistakes because I'm human."
- "I am good enough and worthy of the best."
- "I learn from my mistakes."
- "I know I can accomplish anything I set my mind to."
- "I am strong."
- "I live each day to the fullest."
- "I make the best of every situation."
- "I am stronger because of my past." (This one is especially useful if you start to dwell on bad

things that have happened in the past.)

- "I have control over my thoughts, feelings, and decisions."
- "I accept the things I cannot change."
- "I accept others for who they are." (This can be useful when dealing with a toxic or trying person.)
- "I can get through this!"
- "I know what I need to do."
- "I can make a difference."
- "I am beautiful and unique."
- "I try to be the best I can be."
- "I will give this my all."
- "I will make this work."
- "I will continue living, no matter what!"
- "I value myself and my life."
- "I love myself."
- "I love everyone in my life for who they are."
- "I have the patience to accept what I cannot change and the courage to change what I am able to."
- "I'm the best person for this [task, position,

date, etc.]."

- "I am open-minded."
- "This will not get the best of me."
- "This is only temporary."
- "This is my life, my rules." (This one is ideal when someone tries to infringe on your boundaries or make a decision for you.)

Eliminate Procrastination

Procrastination is what you do when you lack motivation or confidence to tackle something. You anticipate its unpleasantness, so you try to sweep it under the rug. One thing I found helpful for procrastination is to repeat "Carpe diem!" to myself. Latin for "Seize the day," this phrase is a great mantra to have when you are battling procrastination.

Focus On The Problems Procrastination Creates

I also like to focus on why procrastination actually creates more problems for me in the long run. For instance, if I put off paperwork for too long, it will accumulate and become even more of an arduous task. Getting it done now will make things easier for me.

Realize that procrastination will only make you miss a deadline. Use the impending fear of hearing anger from your boss or even losing your job if you don't get something done as motivation.

Focus On The Positive

Another helpful way to think about procrastination is to focus on the reward awaiting you when you get something done. Imagine the confidence and accomplishment you feel. Now you are free to move on to more enjoyable tasks, without the threat of the tasks you are putting off looming over your mind. Furthermore, you can finish your work for the day, feeling satisfied. You can go home and not worry about what you have put off.

Always give yourself a reward to look forward to. Once you complete the task you were putting off, treat yourself with a favorite activity. This reward should be substantial enough to motivate you. A massage, a day of golf, your favorite dessert – these are all good motivators.

Remove the element of dread from the equation. You probably put something off because you don't want to do it. You hate the task or feel that you don't have the strengths to complete it. But if you focus on the positives of the task, then you will hate it less. Think about what good it will do you or the good things that may arise while you perform the task. Talk to yourself positively about your tasks. "This is a good thing to be doing right now," is a good positive affirmation for this situation.

Often, if you hate something, you like to say so. You say so to yourself and out loud. All of your co-workers and friends know how much you hate certain things. But you can restructure this thinking by speaking about it positively. When you want to say, "I hate doing dishes!" say "I love dishes!" instead. It may feel cheesy and fake at first, but your words will make a difference in your mind's perception of the task. Then you will feel more motivated to get started.

Treat It As A Step

The task you put off is probably just a small step toward a bigger goal. Perhaps your goal is to recruit ten new clients, but you hate making phone calls. Consider phone calls a small but essential step in achieving the ultimate goal.

When you focus on the goal your task is a part of, you tend to see the purpose of the task. Your brain regards it as important. Therefore, you don't want to put it off.

Your ultimate goal is also a viable distraction. Instead of treating this task as a huge insurmountable challenge, you feel distracted by the knowledge that it is just a part of a bigger picture. You shrink your mind's catastrophic magnification of the task so that you feel less horrible about it, and you become more devoted to the overall goal. The pay-off of the work will also appear like a reward to motivate you even more.

Repeat, Repeat, Repeat

Consistency is key in self-talk. In his book *The Psychology of Influence and Persuasion,* Robert Cialdini talks about influencing people with commitment and consistency [26]. The fact of the matter is, you can influence yourself with this same principle of influence.

To influence yourself, you must understand the concepts at work behind commitment and consistency. When you commit to something, your brain becomes partial to it. Your brain is likely to stay consistent and follow something through. Therefore, consistent repetitions of positive self-talk can make your brain commit to positive self-talk, and in turn, it chooses to stick to that habit throughout your life.

Repeating positive self-talk every day needs to start as a conscious practice. Your habit lies in negative self-talk, so you will have to focus on adjusting that habit to change your brain's commitment. Every time you talk to yourself negatively, create new neural pathways by chasing those thoughts with positive ones. The more you do this, the more your brain will follow the positive self-talk track without even bothering with negative self-talk.

For at least 66 days, make a time commitment to this self-work. Sit down with your CBT journal for at least five minutes at the same time each day and analyze the paths your thoughts take, the feelings these thoughts trigger, and what beliefs underlie the thoughts. That way, you can teach yourself new ways of thinking that are far more helpful. After 66 days, this will become such a habit that you may not need to work in your journal every day. You will simply adopt the positive thoughts as a habit and avoid the cognitive distortions that keep you trapped in misery.

You should also repeat positive affirmations to yourself. This drives the ideas you want to keep home. Three times a day is a good way to start using positive affirmations habitually.

Consistently practice in pep talks when you start to feel down. Take some time to tell yourself how great you are and how much you can accomplish. As you inspire your belief in yourself and your confidence, it will get easier to overcome fear and doubt.

Consistently strive to be positive, no matter the situation. As you start to dwell on how terrible something is, remind yourself to focus on the silver lining.

Every single day, think of three things you like about yourself. Also, think of three things you are grateful for in your life. This is a great way to reflect back on your day as you lie down to go to sleep or as you drive to work in the morning, feeling overwhelmed, apprehensive, or lazy. With time, this too will become a habit. You will learn to appreciate yourself and your life more.

It is essential to be consistent in positive self-talk. When you make it a habit, you will do it subconsciously, and positive things will happen automatically. To automate the process, make a commitment to positive self-talk and practice it every day until it becomes a part of your brain.

Conclusion

Negative self-talk is one of the worst habits that human beings engage in. Unfortunately, your environment, background, and self-beliefs drive this habit. Your mind sticks to negative thinking because that is the easiest thing for it to do. Changing can take some time and work, but it is absolutely worth it.

When you evict the cruel critic in your mind, you open up your life for new and great things. You stop letting yourself drown in fear and insecurity. Your renewed motivation and confidence will fuel vigor for life. As a result, your problems resolve and you have a better work, social, and family life.

Contrary to what many people think, life and other people are not out to get you. The real culprit to your misery, depression, and personal problems is your problematic thinking. Using techniques to reprogram your subconscious, you can essentially reroute your thinking and become a much happier person. The power lies within you to have anything you want. You just have to break down the barriers and rules that your negative thinking erects around you.

Using positive self-talk involves a lot of repetition to reprogram your subconscious mind. You can also use mindfulness meditation to strengthen your mental mastery. Pep talks before a big event or performance can motivate you. Unlocking the flow state is essential for getting work done really well and achieving total concentration and dedication to a task.

As you use these techniques, you start to achieve a habit of positive thinking. While it takes time to perform this programming and build a new, healthy habit, the work is certainly worthwhile. The rewards you receive in the end are priceless.

You should always use positive self-talk on your family. It will foster a more positive home environment. As you teach your kids positive thinking, you will feel like a better parent. You will also be a better spouse as you talk to your husband or wife kindlier.

Positive self-talk is a secret known by many successful people in business. They often engage in positive self-talk without even knowing it; positive self-talk is simply a habit that they are used to. These people do experience fear and doubt, just like any other person, but they use positive thinking to overcome these difficulties. By improving your self-talk, you can make your work environment and performance better, so that you can get those raises or promotions you have been yearning for. You can also find the motivation to get through daunting or tedious tasks. You can unlock the confidence to venture out and start your own business or make a bold career move.

Positive self-talk also grows your social circle. As you

begin to project positivity, more people will enjoy being around. Cue more dates and more friends! You can even overcome shyness by talking yourself up.

The basic key to positive self-talk is talking to yourself like you would a dear friend. Build yourself up and encourage yourself in all areas of life. You deserve to be happy. So, stop letting your negative thinking chip away at your joy, and instead love yourself!

References

[1] Kross, Ethan, et al. *Self-Talk as a Regulatory Mechanism: How You Do It Matters.* Journal of Personality and Social Psychology. American Psychological Association. 2014. Vol. 106, No. 2, 304–324. DOI:10.1037/a0035173

[2] Gardner, Benjamin, et al. *Making Health Habitual.* British Journal of General Practice. 2012. Vol 62, No 605, pp. 664-666.

[3] Bridge, DJ, & Paller, Ken. *Neural Correlates of Reactivation and Retrieval-Induced Distortion.* Northwesten Medicine. Journal of Neuroscience. Vol 32, Issue 35, pp. 12144-12151. DOI: https://DOI.org/10.1523/JNEUROSCI.1378-12.2012.

[4] Williams, Paul, et al. *Serotonin Disinhibits a Caenorhabditis elegans Sensory Neuron by Suppressing Ca^{2+}-Dependent Negative Feedback.*

Journal of Neuroscience. 21 February 2018. Vol. 38, Issue 8, pp. 2069-2080. DOI: https://DOI.org/10.1523/JNEUROSCI.1908-17.2018

[5] Wolf, Alex. *Cognitive Behavioral Therapy: An Effective Practical Guide for Rewiring Your Brain and Regaining Control over Anxiety, Phobias, and Depression.* ISBN13: 9781726691222.

[6] Goodhart, D. *Some psychological effects associated with positive and negative thinking about stressful event outcomes: was Pollyanna right?* Journal of Personal Social Psychology. Vol 48, Issue 1, pp. 216-232. DOI: https://www.ncbi.nlm.nih.gov/pubmed/3981389.

[7] Gregoire, Carolyn. *The Brain-Training Secrets of Olympic Athletes.* Huffington Post. https://www.huffpost.com/entry/mind-hacks-from-olympic-a_n_4747755.

[8] Raalte, JV. Et al. *Cork! The Effects of Positive and Negative Self-Talk on Dart Throwing Performance*. Journal of Sport Behavior. 1995. Vol 18, Issue 1.

[9] O'Doherty, J., et al. *Beauty of a Smile: The Role of the Medial Orbitofrontal Cortex in Facial Attractiveness*. Neuropsychologica. 2003. Vol. 41, pp. 147-155. https://pure.mpg.de/rest/items /item_2614428/component/file_2623264/content

[10] Brown, Kirk, et al. *Mindfulness: Theoretical Foundations and Evidence for Its Salutary Effects*. Psychological Inquiry. 2007. Pp. 211-237. https://DOI.org/10.1080/1047840070159829 8.

[11] Csikszentmihalyi, Mihaly. *Flow: The Psychology of Optimal Experience*. 2009. Harper Collins. ASIN:

B000W94FE6.

[12] Farber, P. D., Khavari, K. A., & Douglass, F. M. (1980). *A factor analytic study of reasons for drinking: Empirical validation of positive and negative reinforcement dimensions.* JOURNAL OF CONSULTING AND CLINICAL PSYCHOLOGY, *48*(6), 780-781. http://dx.DOI.org/10.1037/0022-006X.48.6.780

[13] Burnett, Paul. *Children's Self-Talk and Significant Others' Positive and Negative Statements.* Educational Psychology. 1996. Vol 6, Issue 1. https://DOI.org/10.1080/0144341960160105

[14] Murayama, Kou. *The Science of Motivation.* American Psychological Association. 2018. https://www.apa.org/science/about/psa/2018/06/motivation.

[15] Pierce, Jon & Gardner, Donald. *Self-Esteem within the Organizational Context*. Journal of Management. 2004. Vol 30, Issue 591. DOI: 10.1016/j.jm.2003.10.001

[16] Conway, Jerome. *Multiple-Sensory Modality Communication and the Problem of Sign Types*. AV Communication. Vol 15, Issue 4, pp. 371-383. https://www.jstor.org/stable/30217403.

[17] Newton, Claire. *The Five Conversation Skills*. Web. N.d. http://www.clairenewton.co.za/my-articles/the-five-communication-styles.html.

[18] Choi, M. *Increase in brain activation due to sub-tasks during driving: fMRI study using new MR-compatible driving simulator*. Journal of Physiological Anthropology. 2017. Vol 36, Issue 11. DOI: 10.1186/s40101-017-0128-8

[19] Cloud, Henry & Townsend, John. *Safe People: How to Find Relationships that are Good for You and Avoid Those That Aren't.* 2016. Zondervan Publishing. ISBN-13: 978-0310345794.

[20] Carney, DR., Cuddy, A., & Yap, A. (2010). *Power Posing: Brief Nonverbal Displays Affect Neuroendocrine Levels and Risk Tolerance.* Psychological Science, Vol 1-6, DOI: 10.1177/0956797610383437

[21] Ko, Sei, et al. *The Sound of Power: Conveying and Detecting Hierarchical Rank Through Voice.* 2014. Psychological Science. ttps://DOI.org/10.1177/0956797614553009.

[22] Chapman University. New Research on Attractiveness and Mating. ScienceDaily. https://www.sciencedaily.com/releases/2015/

09/150916162912.htm.

[23] Elliot, A. J., Tracy, J. L., Pazda, A. D., & Beall, A. T. (in press). *Red enhances women's attractiveness to men: First evidence suggesting universality.* Journal of Experimental Social Psychology.

[24] Carolyn Parkinson, Adam M. Kleinbaum, & Thalia Wheatley. *Similar neural responses predict friendship.* Journal of Nature Communications, Vol 9, Article # 332. 2018.

[25] Cascio, Christopher, et al. *Self-affirmation activates brain systems associated with self-related processing and reward and is reinforced by future orientation.* 2015. Social Cognition Affect Neuroscience. Vol 11, issue 4, pp. 621-629. DOI: 10.1093/scan/nsv136.

[26] Cialdini, R. (2008). *Influence: The Psychology of Persuasion, 5ᵗʰ Ed.* Allyn and Bacon. ISBN-13: 9 78-0061241895

Disclaimer

The information contained in this book and its components, is meant to serve as a comprehensive collection of strategies that the author of this book has done research about. Summaries, strategies, tips and tricks are only recommendations by the author, and reading this book will not guarantee that one's results will exactly mirror the author's results.

The author of this book has made all reasonable efforts to provide current and accurate information for the readers of this book. The author and its associates will not be held liable for any unintentional errors or omissions that may be found.

The material in the book may include information by third parties. Third party materials comprise of opinions expressed by their owners. As such, the author of this book does not assume responsibility or liability for any third party material or opinions.

The publication of third party material does not constitute the author's guarantee of any information, products, services, or opinions contained within third party material. Use of third party material does not guarantee that your results will mirror our results. Publication of such third party material is simply a recommendation and expression of the author's own opinion of that material.

Whether because of the progression of the Internet, or the unforeseen changes in company policy and editorial submission guidelines, what is stated as fact at the time of this writing may become outdated or inapplicable later.

written expressed and signed permission from the author.

CPSIA information can be obtained
at www.ICGtesting.com
Printed in the USA
BVHW030233301120
594464BV00012B/145